Contents

Foreword

'The great advantage of this easy-to-read guide is that its author, though an experienced and well-informed medical journalist, is not a doctor. He thus writes in exactly the clear, non-technical way that typical members of the public need. What's more, himself being in the age group most affected by prostate disease, he discusses the often difficult and emotional issues involved, with the sensitivity and empathy that all too often are missing from treatment and care. I am therefore very happy to recommend *Prostate Cancer – The Essential Guide* to the widest possible public.'

Urologist Dr. Tom Stuttaford, vice chairman of Prostate UK and leading campaigner for better awareness of and improvement in the treatment of prostate cancer.

Introduction

Sooner or later, nearly every man will need to know more about his prostate than when, in his youth, he took it for granted – or didn't even realise that he had one.

The prostate gland, though not essential for an individual's life, is essential for life itself, for reproduction. It produces vital nutrients and fluid which nourishes and protects semen, the milky liquid that transports sperm. Clearly, then, it's a men-only organ.

But this book is not for men only. Women too – wives, partners, girlfriends, mothers even – are as much concerned about prostate cancer as the men they love and care for. They need to know what prostate cancer and other prostate problems mean, not only for the affected man but also for them.

Doctors too, of course, have a crucial role. So have nurses and other carers. NICE, the National Institute for Health and Clinical Excellence, insists that healthcare professionals 'should support men, but also their partners or carers in making treatment decisions'.

Actually, there is more to it than that, especially for doctors, and it would be nice to think that some will read this. While cancer patients these days expect better communication with doctors, and doctors are (in theory at least) trained to be more considerate and sensitive in the way they talk to patients, many still are often bad in the way they do so.

Good communication is an essential part of good treatment because a well-informed patient is likely to get the best benefit from it. With cancer, that isn't easy. 'To put across the real meaning of tests and other information is often as difficult as performing surgery,' says the European Prostate Cancer Coalition, whose aim is to increase awareness of prostate cancer in Europe.

'If things are done well when doctors communicate the diagnosis, everything will be easier for both them and the medical team. The presence of a nurse can make a big difference.

'The patient should be told he can bring his partner or caregiver with him to the first consultation and have the chance to see the report in advance. And doctors must take time to discuss any questions the patient may have.'

Spider's web

We all know that there are countless sources of information about prostate cancer on the Internet and there's little in this book that isn't there. The best and most useful are detailed in the help list. The web is aptly named: like a spider's web, it catches prey. Yes, it provides masses of information, but some is scholarly or hard to understand, some cranky or liable to mislead, some confusing and some outdated. It can be bewildering, and, after all, information isn't necessarily knowledge! That apart, some older men and women – the age groups most affected by prostate cancer – prefer not to use computers, don't like to rely on them, or simply don't have one.

Newspaper reports must be treated with caution too. Many are excellent yet, almost daily, the press runs stories about some 'breakthrough' which is, in reality, nothing of the kind. The hope is hyped.

This book, by contrast, reliably, clearly and concisely says all you need to know in an understandable, easy-to-read format. Its main message is simple: although prostate cancer is the most common cancer in British men, accounting for a quarter of all new male cancer diagnoses (about 36,000 new cases a year) usually it takes it easy; many prostate cancers are so slow-growing that they have little or no effect on health, even without treatment.

Although some 10,000 men die from the disease each year in the UK – one every hour – most do so only after many fulfilling years since being diagnosed and the great majority die from something else, or simply old age. Clearly, getting prostate cancer is not a death sentence.

More than half (57%) of the affected men are over 70. The disease is uncommon below 50. Age, then, is the main risk, though there are others; chapter 1 looks at them all.

The enlarged prostate can press on the urethra, the outlet from the bladder, where urine is stored until released. That can result in uncomfortable, annoying or embarrassing difficulties of one kind or another when peeing. None of these necessarily means cancer because the prostate's enlargement may be – and in fact, usually is – not cancerous. Later in the book, chapter 8 deals with those other conditions, called 'benign' – not because they're gentle, mild or neutral, they aren't! – but because they're not 'malignant' (i.e. not cancerous: they won't spread).

After tests for prostate cancer in chapter 3 and diagnosis in chapter 4, treatments are described and discussed in chapter 5. After treatment, even if it's radical, life can be long, fruitful and happy. But, of course, difficulties can arise. Chapter 6 considers prognosis – how things are likely to go in the future – including such possible complications as bone cancer should the original prostate cancer spread.

'Fitness can fight cancer' is the motto of chapter 7, which shows how sensible nutrition and regular exercise can speed recovery after surgery and help maintain health thereafter. Concluding chapters detail other prostate conditions with symptoms like cancer which are not malignant and outline current research into new and better treatments. At the end of the book there's a handy help list and glossary, which I hope proves helpful.

Some people get the word 'prostate' wrong and talk about 'prostrate cancer'. The best answer to that is: 'Don't take it lying down!' (pun intended). The key point, and never forget it, is that many men, and probably most men with prostate cancer, die *with* it, not *of* it. Overall, indeed, only 3% die of prostate cancer itself.

Your best chances depend, crucially, on being open with your closest loved ones and with your doctor or practice nurse. There's no need to be embarrassed. Don't be slow or shy in asking about any aspect of your condition and its consequences. Even if you don't have any symptoms of the disease, but are concerned about prostate cancer, be aware that you have a right to ask your GP for a PSA blood test – an early indicator of possible prostate problems – and to be given balanced advice about its pros and cons. 'Visit a GP at once if you have any problem "down under", however embarrassing,' declared impresario Andrew Lloyd Webber, after being successfully treated for prostate cancer.

John Neate, chief executive of The Prostate Cancer Charity, warns likewise. 'Too many men put off going to their GP if they develop symptoms because of fear of a prostate cancer diagnosis. It's amazing how many are prepared to accept uncomfortable symptoms as normal and simply not visit their doctor.'

Disclaimer

This book is for general information on prostate cancer and can be used alongside professional medical advice, but it is not intended to replace professional medical advice.

Chapter One

About the Prostate
and Prostate Cancer

Though not essential for an individual man's life, the prostate gland is essential for life itself, because without it reproduction would be impossible. From the prostate come vital nutrients and fluid which nourish and protect semen, the milky liquid from seminal vesicles in the groin that transports sperm.

The healthy prostate is deep in the pelvis, very near the lower end of the bowel, and is wrapped round the neck of the bladder like a doughnut. When healthy, it's firm, like the end of your nose, and is shaped like a walnut but slightly larger. It weighs about four ounces (11 grams) but can be up to half as large again.

Divided into two lobes, it's made of glands and muscle surrounded by compressed fibrous tissue. Passing through it is the urethra, the bladder outlet, a tube through which both urine from the bladder and semen are discharged from the penis.

In almost all men, like the nose and ears in many cases, the prostate does gradually get bigger with age. That in itself, although it's as common as grey hair, can cause problems, but not necessarily prostate cancer. Its location is the bugbear – it's perilously close to key organs, the bowel and bladder, as well as the nerves on each side which are involved in erection of the penis.

If it's not firm but feels squishy when examined, it's probably infected. If it's hard, it suggests cancer.

So much for the prostate itself. But what about prostate cancer?

Like all other kinds of cancer, prostate cancer develops when the growing process of its millions of cells – the basic units of its life – goes berserk.

'Many prostate cancers are so slow-growing that they have little or no effect on health, even without treatment.'

There has been huge progress recently in understanding the genetic content of cancer cells and that, eventually, might revolutionise treatment. But so far, no one really knows what turns the growing process on and off. If you cut your finger, new cells grow to heal the wound but they don't go on and on growing. With cancer, they do – the cells don't 'know' when to stop growing.

With prostate cancer, they can grow rapidly and some men will die from the disease. But more usually, growth is slow – so slow, indeed, that there are few, if any, symptoms and life expectancy is not affected. Many with prostate cancer will eventually die from other diseases, or simply old age.

Moreover, although cancer is one of the most doom-laden words in the English language, the fact nowadays is that it is usually treatable and, more often than ever in the past, curable. That particularly applies to prostate cancer. It is indiscriminate and silent and it strikes whatever a man's state of health generally or social background. Despite that, recent years have seen huge improvements in the prospects for prostate cancer patients.

'Three out of four men with advanced prostate cancer may soon be able to look forward to years of worthwhile, active life,' says leading authority Dr. Tom Stuttaford, who himself developed an aggressive prostate cancer as long ago as 1999. According to Cancer Research UK, more than six out of 10 men with prostate cancer can expect to live for 10 years compared with only one in five in the 1970s.

Even so, being diagnosed with prostate cancer can change your life, and the lives of family members, in many ways. And it can require many difficult decisions about treatments and lifestyle.

> 'Three out of four men who develop advanced prostate cancer may soon be able to look forward to years of worthwhile, active life.'

Uncontrollable cell growth

Prostate cancer is, actually, a slightly misleading term. That's because it usually consists of several small tumours or pre-cancerous 'PIN' cells dotted about the prostate, rather than a single growth. This is important because it affects treatment. Removing only part of the prostate, for example, is seldom an option.

Cancer develops in the prostate when some of its cells grow uncontrollably. Normally, most of them divide, mature and die in a steady, regulated process. But cancer cells, instead of dying, keep on forming new and abnormal cell growths – tumours. Most prostate cancer cells come from the lining of the gland, a type of cancer known as adenocarcinoma.

High cure rate

The first prostate tumour that develops can usually be removed or killed. If it's detected early, the cure rate nowadays can be as high as 90%. A generation ago, it was only 67%. The earlier cancer is caught, the better the outlook. But several other factors affect survival – tissue type, where precisely within the prostate the tumour or tumours are, what treatment you get and, of course, how good that treatment actually is.

The trouble is that at this early stage, detection is difficult because tumours are so tiny and often cause hardly any symptoms – perhaps none at all. Prostate tumours can, in some cases, take many years to grow to a detectable size or cause symptoms.

In a few cases, sadly, the cancer is aggressive and grows rapidly. Even then, it's treatable. But untreated, it's not just that tumour cells are more likely than not to grow: they might spread – the process known as metastasis.

Cancer can spread

Then, cancer cells break off and migrate through the bloodstream and the lymphatic system (the body's drainage network to other parts of the body, mostly the bones) causing new tumours in areas near the prostate, in the groin or rectum (back passage), in the spine or ribs or, indeed, more distant organs such as the liver or kidneys. Cure rates then plummet. And it's hard to be sure which cancers will grow slowly and which aggressively, so treatment decisions can be tricky.

Plenty of risk factors

What causes prostate cancer? Good question! No one really knows the answer. 'It is perhaps the most enigmatic malignancy in men,' says NICE, the National Institute for Health and Clinical Evidence. 'Although only 3% of men die from it, almost all would die with it being present if they lived long enough.'

To a great extent, it's a matter of luck, or bad luck. But what the experts can say is that there are risk factors – particular traits, characteristics, qualities, habits, environmental influences – that might increase the risk.

There's no exact figure on risk. In the UK, about 1 in 10 men will get prostate cancer at some time in their lives.

Simply getting older is the main factor. Family history can play an important part. So might a faulty gene, and hormones. Black skin colour might pose extra risk. Lots of fatty food might too.

These and other possible causes are fully discussed in chapter 3, which considers in detail how men might protect themselves against risk factors for prostate cancer.

Summing Up

- Without the prostate, situated deep in the male pelvis, reproduction would be impossible.

- The prostate gradually gets bigger with age. That can cause problems, but not necessarily prostate cancer.

- The causes of prostate cancer are still far from fully understood. By and large, it's down to luck.

- Simply getting older is the main factor.

- Men with a family history of the disease, or who have inherited a faulty gene, or are black, are at higher risk.

- A high-fat diet might be tempting providence.

- Although the prostate enlarges over time in all men, only one in ten gets prostate cancer. Cure rates are high.

Chapter Two

Symptoms of Prostate Cancer

What are the symptoms?

Perhaps the title of this chapter should really be 'What Might be the Symptoms?' That's because most of the many symptoms that can occur might also be warning signs of some other problem – perhaps in the prostate but possibly elsewhere, like the bladder, bowel, kidneys, perhaps with the nervous system, or perhaps because of a chronic condition such as diabetes.

The big problem, more often than not, is that there are no warning symptoms of prostate cancer at all until it's very far advanced, perhaps too far advanced to treat successfully.

The main reason for this is that the disease usually develops very slowly. It can take years, even decades, for the initial tiny and few malignant cells to show. For most of its course, the growth is too small to be noticeable.

What's more, the symptoms which the enlarged gland causes as it squeezes the urethra are not usually due to cancer. Often they arise from one of the so-called 'benign' (i.e. non-cancerous) conditions detailed in chapter 9. Besides that, the symptoms which may give a clue to an underlying disorder vary from person to person and there can be several at once.

All this adds to the uncertainties of diagnosis: it poses quite a puzzle for doctors. That's why preventative checks are crucial. Especially after the age of 50, men should ask their GP for a routine annual check. If you wait for

'Usually, there are no early warning symptoms of prostate cancer.'

symptoms, you wait too long. The doctor will perform a digital rectal exam (DRE) of the prostate and might order a test for prostate specific antigen (PSA), a key marker for prostate cancer – these tests are detailed in chapter 4.

The symptoms of an enlarged prostate that might (or might not!) be signalling a growing cancer fall into two main groups, 'storage' problems and 'obstructive' or 'voiding' problems.

'Storage' problems

'Storage' problems can be summed up by the term 'jumpy' bladder. Symptoms include:

- Frequency of urination.
- Urgency to 'go'.
- Leaking.

Frequency of urination

The need to pee comes more and more often. The need to be near a toilet can restrict many normal activities, not least social life and, even when you're asleep, you can be woken by the need to pee (nocturia).

Urgency to 'go'

Before the age of 40 or so, the normal bladder can hold about a pint of urine. The need to 'go' may become strong, but at that age, it's controllable. In middle age though, the prostate starts to grow. Wrapped round the urethra, it tightens and narrows it so, over time, the bladder gradually takes longer to empty. Sometimes, you can't hold back.

Leaking

Getting up in the morning can trigger the bladder so strongly that it leaks before you reach the loo, so can turning on a tap or even turning the key in the front door might make a loo visit urgent. You might leak when you cough, sneeze or laugh. Annoyingly, at any time of day the need to pee can become uncontrollable. The result is involuntary leaking.

'Obstructive' or 'voiding' problems

- Poor emptying.
- Poor flow.
- Spraying.
- Dribbling.

Poor emptying

Sometimes, a man needs to pee again almost immediately after he thinks he's finished. That's because, over time, the bladder wall becomes less elastic and loses tone, so not all the urine flows out. The bladder muscle thickens with age too and becomes less stretchy than it used to be. It can't hold as much urine, so you need to use the loo more often.

Poor flow

Sometimes, you have to wait for the flow to start. Other times, once it does start, it's poor, weak or interrupted or takes ages to finish. You can help improve this with exercises that strengthen the pelvic floor muscles (see chapter 7). Constipation may also restrict the flow.

Spraying

Because the urethra has become dry overnight, the stream may spray or go in one direction or the other. Or, for added nuisance value, it can be forked and exit, usually inconveniently, in unintended directions, typically first thing in the morning. This almost always corrects itself once urine flows and opens up the urethra.

Dribbling

Lots of dribbling at the end of the stream is usually due to an obstruction – perhaps an enlarged prostate, perhaps a narrowing of the urethra or the meatus (the opening at the end of the penis). But another common cause is not medical at all, merely zippered flies. Totally free flow can be impeded by the bottom edge of the fly pushing on the urethra. The 'cure' is simple: gently close the meatus to direct the flow, or drop the trousers and sit down to pee. If mild dribbling persists, 'milk' the urethra and pat dry. If the problem remains or gets worse, then see your doctor.

'Home remedies are inadvisable for treating possible symptoms of an enlarged prostate.'

Other problems

The following problems don't necessarily mean cancer, but they should all be checked out by your GP without delay. Treatment with home remedies is inadvisable.

- Pain when urinating.
- Blood in the urine.
- Retention.
- Bone pain.
- Sexual problems.

Pain or burning sensation when urinating

Pain or burning sensation when urinating (also known as dysuria) is probably caused by infection. Stones in the bladder or kidneys might be responsible. Prostate cancer can't be ruled out, but it is the least likely cause.

Blood in the urine

Blood in the urine (also known as haematuria) isn't always visible to the naked eye, another reason why regular annual checks are advisable. There are many possible causes. Again, prostate cancer is the least likely. Blood in the urine might simply be due to an enlarged prostate without cancer. Or it could be a bladder or kidney problem. Some chronic conditions such as diabetes, high blood pressure or damage to the nerves that control the bladder might be at work. In many cases, the cause remains a mystery.

Acute urine retention

You need to pee but, perhaps suddenly, you can't. The tummy swells and it's very painful. There are many possible causes but only one of them is prostate enlargement. Constipation can cause retention as can allowing the bladder to become too full. Cold weather might play a part. Also, some drugs could be responsible, especially diuretics, which are (ironically) designed to remove excess fluid from the body. Often, again, no particular cause can be identified. The important thing with retention is to see your GP as soon as possible or call an ambulance.

Bone pain

Any bone or joint pain should be checked out by your GP at once. Pain is likely when prostate cancer has metastasised (spread) to the bones, especially in the spine, hips or limbs, or maybe in the head, shoulders or the pelvis. Even though the cancer has already taken hold, such pains might be the first really noticeable symptoms of it.

Often, bone pain will come and go. In advanced cases, it can be intractable, disabling and demoralising. There might also be more generalised aches and pains, along with weakness and fatigue. But here again, unless especially severe, such problems might, even now, be due merely to the all-too-natural process of getting older.

Sexual problems

Sexual problems can sometimes occur because of prostate enlargement.

- It may become difficult to get an erection or, perhaps, erections become less rigid than usual because the growth of the prostate is stemming blood flow into the penis.

- Ejaculation may become painful because urethral constriction narrows the channel through which the semen passes.

- There might be blood in the semen (haematospermia). This might give it a brownish or red colour, but often it isn't visible to the naked eye at all and will only show up from a doctor's examination. In about 20% of cases, the condition is 'self-limiting', with just one episode and no recurrence. Of the many possible causes, prostate cancer is the least likely.

- Impotence – inability to sustain an erection sufficient for sexual intercourse – may indicate prostatic disease.

- Less semen during ejaculation than usual may be due to prostate disease, though it is not necessarily prostate cancer.

Annual check-ups

For safety's sake and peace of mind, see your GP about any symptom that concerns you and attend annual check-ups.

If indeed you do have prostate cancer, you won't have all the above symptoms – you might not even have any. However, the symptoms listed here can equally not lead to a prostate cancer diagnosis because they're not specific to prostate cancer. That is, the same symptoms can be, and usually are, caused by conditions other than prostate cancer itself. But better to be safe than sorry.

Summing Up

- Sometimes there are no warning symptoms of prostate cancer at all until it has spread.

- Most possible symptoms might not be warning signs of prostate cancer itself but some other problem.

- Symptoms fall into two main groups – storage and obstructive. Sexual and other problems can also occur.

- Especially after the age of 50, you should have annual checks.

Chapter Three
Preventing Prostate Cancer

What does prevention really mean?

Preventing prostate cancer means doing what it takes to lower the chance of the disease occurring and to reduce the risk of premature death. There are two main ways that might help to prevent prostate cancer:

- Avoiding or minimising risk factors.

- Increasing preventive factors by changing diet specifically and lifestyle generally

Risk factors

These are the traits and habits which increase the risk of disease, outlined in chapter 1. To prevent new cancers from starting, doctors and scientists look at them carefully, but they aren't the whole story. Many people with risk factors never get prostate cancer. And other men without any known risk factors do sometimes develop it. The risk factors include:

- Age.

- Family medical history.

- Ethnic origin.

- Faulty genes.

- Smoking.
- Alcohol.
- Diet.
- Hormones.
- Other factors.
- Postcode.

Age

Age is top of the risk list – the older you are, the greater the risk. Prostate cancer before 40 is rare, with two-thirds of prostate cancers being found in men over 65. The risk in younger men is only one in 500 and few men under 50 develop prostate cancer. But among the over-70s, it develops in more than half. Almost all men, if they lived to be 100, would have prostate cancer.

Family medical history

Medical history is second only in importance to age as a risk factor and can pose a risk because prostate cancer seems to run in some families. If any close relatives – a father or, particularly, a brother – have had prostate cancer, risk is double the average; if they were diagnosed before they reached 60, the risk rises a little more. And if two or more close relatives have had the disease, the risk is greater still. Even so, inherited prostate cancer occurs in only 5-10% of cases.

Ethnicity

Different races around the world have different rates of prostate cancer. The disease affects three times more African, Caribbean and mixed race men than white or Asian men.

The reasons are unclear because so many constantly changing influences might play a part, particularly environment and diet. For instance, prostate cancer is uncommon in Japan, but much more common in the West, even among Japanese men who live in the West. African and Caribbean men have the highest incidence; white men come next. Indian and Pakistani men living in Britain have a higher risk than white men; Chinese and Bangladeshi men are at lower risk. Here again, no one is sure why.

Faulty genes

The fact that close relatives with prostate cancer increase risk suggests that faulty genes might be the culprit. Cancer Research UK scientists have identified seven of these and there are probably more (see chapter 9).

One might have been inherited if several women in the family have had breast cancer. The BRCA2 gene especially, but BRCA1 also, both increase the chances of getting breast cancer and seem to carry a higher risk of prostate cancer too. More research is needed to understand the role of these wayward genes and see what can be done about them. But they're unlikely to account for more than a few cases.

Smoking

Tobacco creates health risks without a doubt and should always be avoided. But there's no solid evidence that, by affecting hormone levels perhaps, or through exposure to substances which can cause cancer (carcinogens), it increases the risk of prostate cancer, as it does with lung and bladder cancers.

Alcohol

Similarly, most studies have shown that risk is not increased by alcohol, although some research does indicate that regular heavy drinking might increase the chances of getting aggressive prostate cancer – tumours that grow or spread quickly.

'There's ignorance of prostate cancer among African and Caribbean men. Lives could be saved if they got themselves tested.'

Diet

What you eat and drink might increase risk, but no one is sure. Healthy eating is, self-evidently, always better than the alternative, but whether diet affects prostate cancer risk is a moot point. Because people eat so many different things, it's so far proved impossible to pinpoint any certain link between diet and cancer.

A huge study of 520,000 people in 10 European countries, including the UK, has been looking for that link, if it exists. Called EPIC (the European Prospective Investigation into Cancer and Nutrition), it has not shown, since starting in 1992, anything more than the risk of prostate cancer is not related to fruit and vegetable consumption.

Some researchers say that a high fat diet, with lots of milk, butter and cheese, cream and red meat, might increase risk; others believe that lack of vegetables, especially cruciferous ones like broccoli, cabbage, cauliflower and sprouts, might be linked to higher risk. But so far it's all a bit vague.

After being treated for prostate cancer, healthy diet becomes doubly important (see chapter 7).

Hormones

Hormones are body chemicals that regulate the activity of various cells and organs, so might play a part in the risk of developing prostate cancer. For instance, the prostate needs the sex hormone testosterone, produced by the testicles, and it was long thought that higher blood levels of testosterone might increase the risk of prostate cancer. But the latest research hasn't proved that link.

Other factors

- Vasectomy, a minor operation to make a man sterile, used to be considered a risk, but isn't any longer.

- Only a few studies indicate that being overweight might be a risk.

- Some research suggests that having an inflamed prostate might raise the risk, but other research has found no such link.

- Research has failed to show that sexual infections, such as gonorrhoea or chlamydia, might increase risk.

- Men with high-grade prostatic intraepithelial neoplasia (PIN), a non-cancerous growth of cells which line the inner and outer surfaces of the prostate, might increase risk. Though not itself malignant, PIN does suggest that undesirable changes are taking place.

Postcode

Prostate cancer risk varies widely, depending on where you live. So says the pressure group Prostate Cancer Charter for Action, which looks at death rates in every parliamentary constituency.

They've found, for instance, that your chances of dying from prostate cancer are almost four times higher in Barnsley, West Yorkshire (37 per 100,000), than in Waltham Forest, Greater London (10 per 100,000). Mid Sussex, the UK's worst performing area, has a rate of 41 deaths per 100,000 people but in nearby Crawley it's only 16. Health officials cannot explain these disparities.

Much uncertainty

How uncertain scientists still are about prostate cancer risk factors is shown in a report by America's authoritative National Cancer Institute on two major studies of folate, a vitamin B nutrient.

One study showed that folate increases the risk. The other showed that folate lowers the risk.

Preventive factors

Besides risk factors, doctors and scientists also look for preventive factors, practices or ways of life which reduce the chances of getting prostate cancer.

Unfortunately, because there's no really clear explanation of what causes prostate cancer, there's no really clear idea of what might prevent it, or at least delay its onset.

'Prostate cancer has no firmly known cause so there's no clear idea of what might prevent it.'

Regular exercise and a healthy diet always make good sense, but the evidence that they might protect against prostate cancer is uncertain. There are no firm nutritional guidelines for prostate cancer prevention.

So, although all kinds of experts are researching all kinds of ways to deal with prostate cancer, there are no 'magic bullets', no sure-fire prescriptions.

Reducing the risks

As there's no really firm explanation of what causes prostate cancer, there's little clear idea of what might prevent it, or at least delay its onset. Some factors that might reduce the risk of developing prostate cancer could include:

- Low-fat diet.
- Lycopene and other antioxidants.
- Selenium and vitamin E.
- Vitamin D.
- Diabetes.
- Exercise and weight.
- Regular sex.
- Painkillers.
- Finasteride.

Low-fat diet

Small portions of a moderate calorie diet, low in dairy produce and red meat (especially barbecued meat) and high in fruit and vegetables, might reduce the risk of prostate cancer.

Nutritionists point to the low incidence of prostate cancer among Japanese men. They think it's thanks to their traditional diet consisting chiefly of soybean products and coldwater fish such as salmon, mackerel, sardines and herring.

Lycopene and other antioxidants

Many experts say that the lycopene in cooked or sun-dried (but not raw) tomatoes, and even more in tomato juice, tomato sauce and tomato paste, or, perhaps better still, with a little alcohol, as in a Bloody Mary, can significantly help to prevent prostate cancer. But that hasn't been shown for sure.

Green tea, red grapes and grape juice, citrus fruit, berries and garlic have also been suggested as they contain antioxidants which might help counter cancer.

Selenium and vitamin E

Some research indicates that protection against cell damage leading to prostate cancer could come from the trace element selenium, found in Brazil nuts, bread, fish and eggs, and also from vitamin E in soya, corn and olive oil, nuts, seeds and wheatgerm in cereals and cereal products. While these are certainly nutritious, cancer experts now say that, according to the latest scientific evidence, neither is likely to help very much against prostate cancer.

Vitamin D

Vitamin D might help ward off prostate cancer, according to some studies. Few foods are rich in vitamin D, but fish liver oil, cheese and egg yolks contain some. Check with your GP to see if you need a vitamin D supplement.

Diabetes

If you have diabetes, you will have a slightly lower risk of prostate cancer than average. No one knows why. It might be something to do with a change in the level of insulin-like growth factor, the body chemical which helps to regulate normal cell growth.

Exercise and weight

More than half of studies which have looked at the effect of exercise on prostate cancer suggest that being more physically active probably reduces prostate cancer risk.

It's also important not to become overweight. Researchers haven't established a direct link between obesity and prostate cancer, but obesity might affect hormones related to risk of getting the disease. Exercise after treatment is especially vital for resuming as normal a life as possible (see chapter 7).

Sexual activity more than 10 times a month by men in their 50s might give 'a small level of protection' against prostate cancer, according to some scientists (see chapter 9)

Masturbation

According to an Australian research group, men in their 20s who ejaculate every day might be less likely to develop prostate cancer later in life (see chapter 9).

Painkillers

Aspirin and anti-inflammatory drugs, like the painkiller ibuprofen, might lower the risk of prostate cancer, according to several research teams. But other research suggests it could increase it. There are also concerns that regular aspirin use might cause life-threatening stomach bleeding.

Finasteride (brand name Proscar), used to treat benign prostatic hyperplasia (BPH), detailed in chapter 8, might prevent prostate cancer according to some urologists. But others say it does no more than shrink tumours which are not life-threatening. It also, misleadingly, lowers the PSA count, which could lead to a dangerous false-negative result (chapter 4).

And finally . . .

Even if you successfully avoid all conceivable risk factors, even if you increase all possible protective factors, there's no guarantee that you won't develop prostate cancer. But at least your risk has a good chance of being less.

Summing Up

■ There are eight main risk factors for prostate cancer. You can do nothing about age, ethnic origin, skin colour, family medical history or, to any significant extent as yet, your genes or hormones. Two you can tackle – smoking and diet.

■ As prostate cancer has no clear cause, there's no clear idea of what might prevent it. But the risk is likely to be reduced by adopting a sensible, balanced lifestyle with a balanced low-fat diet and regular exercise.

■ Some specific substances such as antioxidants and vitamin D might protect against prostate cancer, as well as some painkillers and the drug finasteride.

■ There is no guaranteed way of avoiding prostate cancer.

Chapter Four

Diagnosing Prostate Cancer

Checking saves lives

If you have any of the symptoms detailed in chapter 2, such as frequency or urgency, dribbling or poor flow, pain in or around the pelvic area, or sexual problems, do check them out with your doctor, especially if you're over 50.

Tests aren't perfect and sometimes get things wrong, but they could save your life.

Symptoms don't mean you have prostate cancer, but they might. That's why it's important to get a diagnosis. Early diagnosis means early treatment. Early treatment is more effective than later treatment and it's far more likely to result in cure. Timely treatment, even for the most aggressive prostate cancers, can prolong survival for years. Leave it late and it could have spread.

'Visit your GP at once if you have any problem, however embarrassing,' advises impresario and composer Andrew Lloyd Webber. After early treatment for prostate cancer, he got the all-clear.

Despite this, many men shy away from seeing their GP, yet most tests bring good news. More often than not, the symptoms signal non-cancerous conditions. Most GP surgeries will take a blood sample and send it to a laboratory for the tests although some surgeries can do this on-site.

On the other hand, many men with early prostate cancer have no symptoms at all – all the more reason for regular check-ups from age 50 or so.

'Prostate cancer can be lethal but it can be cured. Timely checks are essential.'

What you should do

If you experience any of the symptoms described in chapter 2, consult your GP – a urine check can test for infection. If that's negative, the GP will carry out a physical examination either in the form of a finger test, or digital rectal exam (DRE), or a test for PSA (prostate specific antigen).

DRE test

First, the GP or nurse will feel the back of the prostate for any hard or bumpy areas and estimate its size. It's undignified, perhaps slightly uncomfortable, but it doesn't hurt.

As you lie on your side with the knees tucked up towards the chest, the doctor or nurse will gently slide a lubricated gloved finger into the rectum (back passage) to feel the prostate.

An enlarged prostate could be a sign of benign prostatic hyperplasia (BPH), a non-cancerous condition (see chapter 8). Hard or irregular areas might suggest prostate cancer and you'll be referred to a hospital specialist.

PSA test

The next step might be a blood test which measures the level of prostate specific antigen (PSA) in the blood. PSA is a protein produced by the prostate to make semen more liquid. The test is quick and simple – a little blood is drawn from a vein in the crook of the elbow with a sterile needle and sent to a lab for analysis.

PSA rises with age. For men in their 50s, a measurement of less than 3.0 ng/ml (nanograms per millilitre) would be normal. For men in their 70s, up to 5.0 ng/ml would be okay.

Although more PSA than normal might mean you have prostate cancer, it probably won't. Only a third, at most, of those with excess PSA have prostate cancer. In fact, most prostate cancers are in men with a normal PSA level. Conditions which aren't cancer, an infection for example, can also increase PSA levels. Some men with prostate cancer may have low PSA, and in a man who's overweight or obese, PSA can be diluted because his blood volume is greater.

Unfortunately, the PSA test can miss cancer (false-negative result) about once in every six cases. Or it can indicate that cancer is there when it isn't (false-positive result). Moreover, the PSA test cannot tell whether the cancer is slow or fast growing. As a result of all of this, one-off tests for PSA are not wholly reliable and more than one check-up is often advisable.

Benefits and downsides of PSA testing include:

- Reassurance if the result is normal, but continuing anxiety and follow-up tests if there have been symptoms.

- Prostate cancer can be found at an early stage but it also can be missed by the test.

- Treatment is likely to extend life even if the cancer is advanced but some men might get unnecessary treatment because the test doesn't show how mild or aggressive the cancer is.

There are three ways to go after a PSA test:

- If the PSA level was normal, you can relax – check again in a year or two.

- If the PSA level is a bit high, it's unlikely you have prostate cancer but further tests might be advisable.

- If the PSA is, in the doctor's view, much too high   and it can go up into the hundreds – you'll be referred to a specialist for a more in-depth investigation and, maybe, a biopsy.

Should you have a PSA test?

The Prostate Cancer Risk Management Programme of the NHS is against routine PSA tests.

'That's because the benefits should always outweigh the harms and there is no clear evidence that they do,' it says. 'That is why the NHS does not invite men who have no symptoms for prostate cancer screening.' Instead, men should seek guidance from their GP.

Dr. Tom Stuttaford sees things differently, 'In countries which give annual PSA testing for men over 50, or over 40 if there's a family history of the disease, the results are far better.'

'Too often, men miss the signs of prostate cancer. They should all get an informed choice about PSA testing, be told its pros and cons and be given access to it if they want.'

Baroness Jan Royall, former health minister.

'You can always press for a test,' he points out, 'If the results are inconclusive (which is common) go for the next stage, ultrasound and biopsy. The latter is uncomfortable and can be a little painful but it's a lot better than the alternative.'

What all this boils down to is, unfortunately, that there's no completely reliable way to be sure which cancers need treatment and which, being harmless, probably don't. While prostate cancer screening definitely saves lives, the jury's still out on whether it does so as effectively as, for instance, screening for breast cancer.

So, talk it over with the your GP or specialist. Get clear information and guidance on the likely benefits and possible harms of testing, investigation and treatment, and their implications. Only ask for a test once you feel it's right for you. Ultimately, the decision is yours.

Further tests

'More tests are needed if initial findings are inconclusive.'

When the results of initial tests are inconclusive, or if they suggest or seem to confirm that cancer is present in the prostate, further tests become necessary. The further tests you're offered could be:

▓ Prostate biopsy (TRUS).

▓ More PSA tests.

▓ Cystoscopy.

▓ Imaging scans.

Prostate biopsy

This procedure, known as TRUS (transrectal ultrasound scan), uses sound to examine the inside of the prostate and will be carried out on you, probably as an outpatient, at your local hospital.

A lubricated finger-sized probe is inserted gently into the back passage. It sends out high frequency sound waves that bounce off the gland to form images on a screen for the specialist to consider.

If need be, a fine needle can be passed through the probe into the prostate to get tiny amounts of prostate tissue for analysis under the microscope. Sometimes it can hurt, but modern anaesthetics are brilliant and can kill most, if not all, pain. The biopsy takes only 10-15 minutes and you can go home soon after.

As with any medical procedure, there are risks. Blood in urine, semen or bowel movements for some weeks is normal and nothing to worry about but in rare cases there can be serious bleeding and infection.

Unfortunately though, as with PSA tests, biopsies can mislead; they can even miss cancer. For example, a negative prostate biopsy means that cancer wasn't detected in the particular parts of the prostate analysed – it doesn't say for sure that there's no cancer elsewhere in the prostate. That's because of so-called 'sampling error'. A needle biopsy collects tissue from a very small area, so a cancerous growth might be missed. Samples from another part might tell a different story.

That could raise the needs for a repeat biopsy, or further tests, and certainly the specialist will want to monitor the situation for some months.

More PSA tests

An initial PSA result of 4-10 ng/mL is sufficiently 'borderline' for the doctor to advise having more tests even after an apparently 'normal' TRUS result.

Some newer types of test for PSA focus on specific aspects, such as its density or how quickly its level rises over time. Another PSA test, still under study, is done with urine rather than blood and shows promise of detecting cancer more reliably and accurately than standard blood screening (see chapter 9).

Doctors differ about how useful such tests are or about when and how they should be used. But the disclosure of an upward trend will suggest – though not confirm – that cancer might well be present. If you had treatment for prostate cancer (chapter 5), PSA testing afterwards can gauge how effective it has been and if cancer has recurred.

Cystoscopy

If an operation is planned, either for prostate cancer or for a urethral constriction due to prostate enlargement, the surgeon can see how healthy or unhealthy the prostate looks like by using a cystoscope.

This is a flexible tube with a lens at the end for viewing. A jelly containing local anaesthetic makes it possible to insert the tube through the urethra with little or no discomfort.

Imaging scans

These investigations, including bone scans, MRI, CT scans and PET scans, are all painless and look at detail inside the body for up to an hour. They're carried out on a couch which slides back and forth through a doughnut-shaped scanner, which takes pictures as you move through it. This is harmless but it does spook some people, making them feel claustrophobic. Hospital doctors and nurses can give all the necessary comfort and reassurance, with perhaps a calming tablet or injection.

The results will come through in a few days though some might take a fortnight. If the results are needed urgently, the doctor will note this on the scan request form.

Bone scan

If PSA is high and because prostate cancer is prone to spread to the bone, you might be advised to have a bone scan in hospital, again probably as an outpatient.

The scan uses an imaging device called a gamma camera to look for changes or abnormalities in bones throughout the body, highlighting 'hot spots' which might be caused by cancer but can also result from injury or arthritis. An initial injection of minimally radioactive material into the bloodstream might hurt slightly.

MRI and CT scans

These are needed when treatment using surgery or radiation is planned and are carried out in hospital. They check for any malignant cells which have spread to the area around the prostate or to the lymph nodes – small round organs in the neck, underarms, chest and tummy trap which help to ward off unwanted bacteria, viruses and cancer cells from the body. MRI – magnetic resonance imaging – uses magnets to align atoms inside the body and measure signals from them which lead to images of tissues and organs. Its main drawback is that it's very noisy, but you'll be given protective headphones.

CT or CAT – computerised (axial) tomography – compiles a series of X-rays taken from different angles to build up a detailed picture of the inside of the body and accurately depicts any tumour.

Early research with one of the later scanning techniques, called diffusion-weighted MRI, show more clearly than ever before which tumours, if any, are growing, according to Professor Nandita deSouza of the Institute of Cancer Research at the Royal Marsden Hospital, London. That would help to limit the number of men who have treatment which turns out not to be necessary.

PET scan

PET – positron emission tomography – shows what body tissues look like and how well they're working. The scanners themselves are very costly and few British hospitals have them, and in any case they are not at present considered suitable in cases of prostate cancer. But research into their possible use goes on (see chapter 9).

Coping with a prostate cancer diagnosis

It's a shock to learn you've got prostate cancer. But finding out what to expect and what to do will ease the fears and anxieties about how you'll cope.

It makes good sense to have as much basic, useful information as you can. Most people forget at least half of what doctors tell them, so if possible, take your wife, partner or a friend with you to the doctor and have a written list of your concerns to ask about. You might want to ask some of the following questions:

▓ Has the cancer spread?

▓ What kind of treatment will I get?

▓ What can I expect during treatment, and afterwards?

▓ What chance is there of cure?

▓ How soon can I get back to work?

▓ What drugs might I get, and what side effects?

▓ What changes in my life can I expect and what should I do about them?

▓ Are there local support groups I could join?

Summing Up

▓ Regular checks after age 50 can save your life, whether you have symptoms or not.

▓ Initial physical examinations are the finger test of the prostate itself and the blood test for PSA, a protein produced by the prostate.

▓ There are both pros and cons for PSA testing. After hearing about these and talking them over with your doctor, the decision to have one or not is your own.

▓ Further tests are advisable if the initial tests are inconclusive or seem to confirm that cancer is present in the prostate.

▓ Besides more PSA tests, possible additional checks include biopsy, using sound; cystoscopy, using direct vision; bone scan, visualising 'hot spots'; and imaging using magnetism or X-rays.

▓ If diagnosed with prostate cancer, together with your wife, partner or a friend, get as much basic, useful information as you can from the doctor and from support groups.

Chapter Five

Treatments for Prostate Cancer

Until the late 1980s, doctors could do little about prostate cancer. They had treatments but all too often these didn't work too well.

Today, it's quite different. There are new ways of detecting prostate cancer early and many more effective treatments, and there are better chances of cure than before – so many, indeed, that the choice now depends on a whole range of factors.

Patient choice

Patient choice is crucial. Because doctors can differ about the best treatment for prostate cancer, and because treatment is considered individually for every man, a lot hinges on the patient himself – his condition, his character and his preferences.

Of course, some men would sooner the doctor made the decisions – and some doctors prefer it that way too. But these days, it's acknowledged that therapy works best when the patient gets the facts from the medical specialist to whom he's been referred by his GP and then himself is actively involved in decisions, with his wife or family alongside. After all, he's the one who has to live with the outcome.

No one can be sure what the future holds and many things need to be taken into account when deciding what treatment to have, so deciding on your treatment can be difficult. Doctors, even cancer specialists, admit they're still not that good at predicting how rapidly a cancer might grow.

The basic considerations are:

- The condition.
- The cancer's nature.
- The doctor's decision.
- The treatment's effects.
- The patient's choice.

Medical organisations in the UK, the rest of Europe and the US all urge medical practitioners who treat prostate cancer to consider treatment for each man individually as no two cases are exactly alike. All men will have individual experiences – you are not going to feel the same way about your condition, or experience side effects in exactly the same way, or get the same outcomes from treatment. For these reasons, if you do receive a diagnosis of prostate cancer, you will play a decisive role in your care and treatment. You must tell your doctors about your needs, your wishes and your concerns.

On top of this, doctors are not all the same and they too might have different views about treatment. As the patient, you should never hold back from getting clear answers to whatever questions you have. Treatment options include the following variables:

- Cancer stage.
- PSA level.
- Gleason score.
- Age and general health.
- Feelings about the treatments.
- When to have treatment.

Cancer stage

Prostate cancer can grow and spread to the nearby lymph nodes or elsewhere in the body. Blood tests, X-rays or CT scans will show if it has and, if so, how far it's got – what stage it's at.

Prostate cancer is staged using the TNM system which assesses the tumour (T), lymph nodes (N) and its spread – metastases (M). Each of these has 10 sub-stages but the basic ones are:

- Stage 1 – the cancer is tiny and completely inside the prostate gland itself, which feels normal in a digital rectal examination (DRE).

- Stage 2 – the cancer is still only inside the prostate but is larger; also a lump or hard area can be felt during a DRE.

- Stage 3 – the cancer has grown into tissue beyond the prostate.

- Stage 4 – the cancer has spread into the bladder or rectum or to the lymph nodes, bones, liver or lungs.

PSA level

As detailed in chapter 4, this varies from man to man and increases with age. Rising PSA readings over time can help to decide whether treatment is needed.

Gleason score

The Gleason score, named after an American pathologist, guesstimates how fast the cancer is likely to grow and spread, based on the shape of the cells and how they're arranged as seen under the microscope – the higher the score, the worse the prognosis.

The Gleason system evaluates the pattern the cancer cells have formed. Tumours can mimic the normal prostate gland pattern and a tumour with almost normal structure will probably itself behave almost normally. But if the pattern of cells in the tumour has few or even no features of the prostate's own structure, it's much more likely to advance rapidly or aggressively.

The appearance of the cancer cells and its pattern are each given a grade from 1-5: the two numbers are added to give a Gleason score. The most usual Gleason scores are 5 (2+3) and 7 (4+3). The lowest possible score is 2, and is seldom seen. The highest is 10, which denotes the most disordered appearance and patterns of prostate cancer cells.

'Treatment is so complicated that it may take more than one visit to the doctor to understand all the options.'

Peter, prostate cancer survivor.

However, men with low Gleason scores sometimes fare poorly; men with high Gleason scores sometimes do well. Prostate cancer is indeed an enigmatic disease, isn't it?

Age and general health

Age and general health matter because prostate cancer often grows very slowly, and the cancer may not even affect general health at all. This means that for a man who's getting on and hasn't any significant prostate symptoms, it might make best sense simply to have check-ups every few months (see 'active surveillance' later on in this chapter).

Not everyone will prefer to 'wait and see' like that but it could be the right choice. That's because the possible side effects of treatment might be worse than the cancer itself, especially if there are other health problems.

'The question
should be:
what's best for
me at this time?'
Dr Sheldon Marks,
US oncologist.

Feelings about the treatments

All treatments are likely to have side effects, occasionally distressing. Many men can put up with urinary incontinence (involuntary urine leakage), for example, but for others such symptoms can seriously damage quality of life. Loss of sexual drive or impotence, likewise, may not matter to some but for others would be intolerable.

If you receive a diagnosis of prostate cancer, what you think and how you feel about the unwanted consequences of treatment is entirely up to you. It's a question of balancing the goals and benefits of therapy against its risks and drawbacks.

There are no 'rights' and 'wrongs' here. It all depends on how you assess the possible benefits and downsides. 'The question should be: what's best for me at this time?' advises American cancer specialist Sheldon Marks.

Unless they can be sure beyond reasonable doubt that treatment will help significantly, many men could quite reasonably continue as normal even though they know they have a potentially lethal disease.

When to have treatment

It's seldom urgent. Of course, no one can guarantee that a prostate cancer won't suddenly start to spread, but a short or medium-term delay is unlikely to make much difference. It's better, certainly, than a snap decision.

If you receive a diagnosis of prostate cancer, you should take time to get the information you need to make a considered choice about how to proceed, to discuss the situation with your wife or partner or family, to weigh the options carefully.

Perhaps you have booked a post-retirement world cruise. Or are about to give your daughter away at her wedding. In such circumstances, it's quite reasonable to postpone treatment for a few weeks or months. But while it's seldom urgent, sometimes it is. There are cases – a high Gleason score, for instance – when delay might lead to early spread whereas quick action could be curative.

Treatment

Prostate cancer is either:

- Localised – contined to the prostate.

- Locally advanced – in the prostate and the surrounding tissues.

- Metastatic – spread to the lymph nodes, bones or other parts of the body.

Which type it is determines whether treatment is:

- Local – removing or destroying the cancer cells.

- Systemic – taken by mouth or by injection.

For localised prostate cancer, the main options are:

- Active surveillance.

- Surgery.

- Radiotherapy.

For more advanced disease, the main options are:

- Radiotherapy.
- Chemotherapy.
- Hormone therapy.

There are also many forms of alternative or unorthodox treatment. These are discussed later in this chapter.

It's important to talk through with the doctor the best treatment for you personally – what might be suitable for other men might not be right for you.

No treatment is without side effects, some serious. Although cancer treatment is carefully planned, it's almost impossible to ensure that cancer cells only are hit and that healthy cells and tissues are not. Unwanted side effects both during and after treatment are all but inevitable. They depend mainly on the type of therapy and its extent, and patients may react differently. But the good news is that side effects can be reduced and even relieved – you should never hold back from telling your doctors, nurses or other carers about any side effects you're feeling.

Also, advises NICE, patients should be offered follow-up appointments after treatment, and their doctor or other healthcare professional should tell them how often and where.

Active surveillance

For some men, the best option may be to have no treatment but just keep a close eye on the situation.

'Active surveillance' means regular monitoring without surgery or other invasive treatment. It's appropriate for older men who have small, low-grade tumours, or slowly rising PSAs. It's also often best for men who have other medical problems which need treatment or whose life expectancy is less than 10 years (provided their prostate cancer isn't large or high grade).

Of course, like any medical intervention, there can be a downside. Although active surveillance won't immediately lead to the physical or sexual complications associated with other treatments, it might increase anxiety.

Even though it's not invasive, like other treatments in this section, active surveillance does mean seeing the doctor regularly and it does entail having PSAs and DREs every 3-6 months as well as fresh biopsies every year or two to make sure the cancer hasn't got worse.

This makes sense because prostate tumours often grow so very slowly. Small, early cancers can take as long as 10 years to cause trouble. Active surveillance may also be recommended when the risks of invasive approaches outweigh the possible benefits.

Surgery

Prostatectomy

A prostatectomy is a surgical operation to remove the entire prostate plus any affected lymph nodes nearby. It is suitable for men who aren't yet 70, or who have low PSA levels or no other significant medical conditions.

Doctors usually remove localised prostate cancer with surgery. There are several ways to do that; there's no certainty about what's best.

The main side effects of all surgery are pain, fatigue and weakness, especially in the first few days afterwards. They can be controlled and you should never be shy about asking for painkillers or other forms of relief.

Prostatectomy may cause permanent impotence, especially in older men. Also, swelling or damage to the muscle that holds urine in the bladder can cause incontinence – minor in about 20% of cases, severe in about 5%.

Some of the latest surgical methods, particularly when removing small tumours, are nerve-sparing, so that impotence or incontinence are only temporary. But after the op, the patient will no longer have a prostate, which means they can't produce semen anymore. However, they can return to having sex and they can still have an orgasm.

'It is the skill of the surgeon that determines the outcome.'
Professor Roger Kirby, urologist.

There are four main types of prostatectomy. Laparoscopic and robotic are 'minimal access', or 'keyhole surgery', techniques.

- Radical retropubic prostatectomy – this is the most common form. The entire prostate and affected lymph nodes near it are removed through a cut in the tummy between the navel and the pubic bone. Pain after surgery can be significant, recovery can be slow and there can be lasting effects on continence and on sexual function and enjoyment. On the other hand, many surgeons say this approach does give a good chance of avoiding incontinence and of sparing the nerves and blood vessels needed for an erection.

- Radical perineal prostatectomy is less invasive than retropubic, with less blood loss and faster recovery. The prostate is removed through a small cut in the perineum, the area between the scrotum and the anus. This operation is sometimes used if the patient is very overweight and cancer is at an early stage, with the lymph nodes unaffected. The chief drawback is that the surgeon can't see and feel the nerves responsible for erections.

- Laparoscopic prostatectomy has several advantages – less pain, less time in hospital, less chance of incontinence afterwards. Greater precision too. Unfortunately, few surgeons yet have enough training and experience to do it. There's also concern that the operation might not clear the cancer thoroughly enough.

- Robotic prostatectomy has been publicised as perhaps the most effective treatment. Using laparoscopic instruments held in a machine, it makes the operation safer and less destructive of tissue around the cancer thanks to its precision and control and there's a faster return to potency and continence. However, the equipment is costly, which has limited its use in the NHS, and the technique is challenging for surgeons, even though their 'learning curve' for it is shorter than laparoscopy.

'It will undoubtedly be those surgeons who take up both laparoscopy and robotic, who will push the boundaries of surgery to the next level,' says Professor Roger Kirby. 'Remember, the robot is nothing more than a surgical tool. It is the skill of the surgeon that determines the outcome.'

Orchidectomy

Orchidectomy is a surgical operation but in effect a hormonal treatment. That's because it removes the testicles, ending production of the male hormone testosterone, which regulates the prostate's growth. Without the testicles, or the active tissues inside them from which testosterone comes, the prostate shrinks.

This operation is most effective. The trouble is that the testicles are so strongly associated with masculinity that it can be really difficult for a man to accept their loss. The operation may be surgically minor, but it's effectively castration. The side effects, too, are often disagreeable. They include loss of sexual drive, impotence and forms of feminisation such as hot flushes and breast growth.

Radiotherapy

External beam radiation therapy

Standard radiotherapy, known as external beam radiation therapy (EBRT), uses high-energy rays or particles to kill cancer cells with radioactive exposure. It is highly effective, increasing survival rates by up to 50%.

Unfortunately, although most patients return to normal within a few weeks of finishing the treatment, as many as a third, maybe even a half, develop long-term bowel problems.

In destroying cancer, the radiation can cause permanent damage to healthy tissue, leading to exhaustion as the body struggles to repair it. Other side effects can be impotence, urination problems, bowel problems, skin irritation and soreness in the back passage.

This is why many of Britain's leading cancer experts, notably Professor Karol Sikora, medical director of CancerPartnersUK, Britain's largest private cancer network, regard EBRT as 'outdated' compared to newer approaches such as conformal and intensity-modulated radiotherapy.

EBRT uses linear accelerators over 3-6 months to destroy small tumours by focusing a beam on the cancer for a few minutes. It's for patients who might not be fit for surgery or, perhaps, prefer it to surgery. In addition, when surgery isn't possible because the cancer has gone beyond the prostate, radiation can lower the chance of the cancer spreading further. Unfortunately, though, it cannot cure it.

Internal radiation therapy

Internal radiation therapy, also known as brachytherapy, attacks cancer of the prostate with strands of rice-sized radioactive seeds planted inside it. This technique is most suited if you have a small, early stage, slow-growing tumour that is confined to the prostate. Its chief advantage is that, because it limits the extent of radiation, the rectum and bladder are protected. Sometimes, hormone treatment is given first, to reduce the prostate's size, as it's difficult to place the seeds properly in a very large prostate.

Conformal radiotherapy

Conformal radiotherapy, unlike standard radiotherapy, is a new approach which images the depth as well as the height and width of tumours. The therapists use a computer to shape the beams of radiation as closely as they can to the shape of the tumour. Working in three dimensions is far more precise and gives a better chance of killing the cancer because it delivers a higher dose of radiation straight to it. It also reduces radiation to surrounding healthy tissue, which minimises side effects.

Intensity modulated radiation therapy

Intensity modulated radiation therapy (IMRT), a type of conformal radiotherapy, focuses shaped beams onto the affected part of the prostate. The dose is adjusted so that the tumour's centre receives most and surrounding tissue gets less. It needs up to 40 exposures every day for eight weeks.

Regrettably, the NHS provides it for fewer than a quarter of those who could benefit from it. Cancer Research UK reports that patients on the continent are twice as likely to receive it as patients in the UK.

Similarly, proton beam therapy, which precisely aims exceptionally powerful subatomic particles onto tumours to minimise harm to other tissues, is not available at all on the NHS for prostate cancer. That is because detailed analysis has concluded it is not cost-effective enough.

Chemotherapy

Drugs are widely used to combat other forms of cancer but for prostate cancer, as a rule, only when it's advanced, recurrent or no longer responding to treatment. It's not advisable to try to boost the immune system with any dietary supplements or herbal medicines while on chemotherapy because they might interfere with its effects.

Like radiotherapy, chemotherapy can become very wearing, chiefly because it can bring on such severe tiredness and loss of energy. This tends to get worse towards the end of treatment and can last for months, but it doesn't last indefinitely. Some drugs can cause numbness, tingling or a burning sensation.

Strangely enough, a little exercise such as a short walk every day can be more helpful than rest. There are many ways to counter fatigue – for example, try not to rush around, have plenty of chairs available, get help from family and friends, and have several small meals a day rather than the standard three.

There are scores of drugs for prostate cancer but the main ones in Britain are listed below. All have side effects. Besides tiredness, the most common are feeling anaemic (washed out or rundown), feeling sick, sore mouth or ulcers, hair loss and proneness to infection because of low white cell blood count. Some drugs have unusual side effects – epirubicin, for instance, can make urine run red – that might be alarming but it's harmless, not blood.

- Docetaxel (brand name Taxotere) is the most commonly used drug licensed in the UK for prostate cancer. It blocks the growth of cancer by stopping the cells from multiplying.
- Paclitaxel (Taxol) works similarly to docetaxel.

- Mitoxantrone (previously called mitozantrone) and epirubicin (Pharmorubicin) are given by drip – through a fine tube into a vein. They block genetic processes so that cancer cells can't divide.

- Estramustine, given as a capsule, is made from a combination of two types of drugs, one containing the hormone oestrogen and the other a cell-killing agent, nor-nitrogen mustard. It prevents tumours from multiplying and blocks hormones which encourage their growth.

Hormone therapy

Hormones, made by various glands in the body, control the growth and activity of cells and organs. Hormone therapy causes the prostate to shrink by depriving it of the male androgen hormones, of which testosterone, produced in the testicles in response to signals from the pituitary gland in the brain, is the most important.

Hormone therapy (including orchidectomy, see page 53) can treat early cancer and high grade tumours very effectively. It's also an option if you can't undergo surgery or radiotherapy, or haven't responded satisfactorily to surgery or radiotherapy, or have a cancer relapse or if the cancer has spread beyond the prostate. It can also supplement radiotherapy or shrink tumours before surgery or radiotherapy to enhance their effects.

The trouble with hormone therapy is that prostate cancers which initially respond to it often become resistant after a year or so. It is, therefore, chiefly used when cancer has spread from the prostate.

Hormonal drugs work only while they are being taken, which means they have to be taken indefinitely. Low levels of male hormones are the chief cause of side effects. The most common problems are:

- Loss of sexual desire or not being able to get or sustain an erection.
- Hot flushes, often made worse by smoking, or drinking tea and coffee.
- Sweats.
- Breast tenderness.
- Weakened bones.

- Diarrhoea.

- Nausea.

- Itching.

- Some men gain weight after hormone treatment.

Half the men on hormone tablets alone experience impotence and all the men on injections become impotent because they stop testosterone production.

LHRH antagonists

LHRH (luteinising hormone-releasing hormone) agonists, also known as pituitary down-regulators, work by stopping the brain from signalling the body to make testosterone, without which prostate cancer cells can't grow. The drugs are given by injections once a month or so into the arm, tummy or bottom, or as a small implant under the skin.

The body's natural response to a first injection is to produce more testosterone and therefore a quicker growth of prostate cancer for a while – a condition called 'flare'. To stop this, doctors often give a short course of anti-androgen tablets a week or so before the first LHRH injection and for a week or two afterwards.

The most commonly prescribed LHRH agonists are goserelin (brand name Zoladex), leuprolin acetate (Prostap), buserelin acetate (Suprefact) and triptorelin (Decapeptyl).

One type of LHRH agonist, histrelin (Vantas) comes as a small plastic cylinder implanted under the skin of the upper arm. It's a palliative treatment – not a cure but only to relieve symptoms – for patients with advanced prostate cancer.

Anti-androgens

Anti-androgens, unlike LHRH agonists, are given as tablets rather than injection, but they do the same job – stopping testosterone from reaching the cancer cells. The main ones are flutamide (brand name Drogenil), bicalutamide (Casodex) and cyproterone acetate (Cyprostat). Their chief advantage is that they minimise or even avoid loss of sexual function, which means a man can still get an erection.

New treatments

New types of treatment are being widely tested in clinical trials. Hundreds of researchers in the UK, the US, Europe and Asia are looking into why cells become malignant and that promises to yield treatments that stop or delay the process.

'But these aren't dramatic breakthroughs,' warns urologist Professor David Kirk. 'They'll help men whose treatment hasn't been wholly or permanently successful but they won't replace standard conventional treatments.'

Gene therapy

'New treatments will improve prostate cancer care but they won't replace conventional treatments.'

Professor David Kirk, UK urologist.

Gene therapy is an experimental approach to change the genetics, the basic make-up, of cancer cells. It might be that the gene which is producing cancer has been damaged in some way, so there might be a vaccine or other therapy to repair it. Or there might be ways to introduce genes that hinder the cancer cells' development, or kill them, or make them easier prey for drugs.

Biological therapies

Biological therapies could help immune systems to stop or slow prostate cancer's growth and prevent it from spreading and might also, researchers say, control the typical and sometimes severe flu-like side effects of biological treatment such as chills, fever, aching, appetite loss, nausea and a tendency to bleed or bruise easily.

Vaccination

Vaccinations of various kinds are under study. Some would target a virus, yet to be identified, which might be a cause, or even *the* cause, of prostate cancer. Others would stimulate the body's immune system to fight off the disease. Still others would try to stifle malignancy in the pre-cancerous stage now managed by active surveillance.

High-intensity focused ultrasound

High intensity focused ultrasound (HFUS) uses high frequency sound waves to wipe out cancer cells. Its chief advantage is that it's non-invasive: it leaves the prostate and the surrounding tissue and nerves intact and in place.

From a probe inserted into the back passage, the pattern of echoes as the sound waves bounce off tissues is converted into an image called a sonogram. This can determine the extent of cancer and see if it's affected surrounding tissues.

HFUS could also prove an accurate tool for tailoring cancer surgery to the individual patient. It has often proved highly effective but there's some way to go yet, mainly due to problems about interpreting the sonograms.

Proton beam radiation therapy

Proton beam radiation therapy (PBRT) targets tumours with streams of positively charged atom particles called protons. According to Dr Kevin Camphausen, a leading American researcher, PBRT has 'wonderful potential' but just how wonderful remains to be seen. Apart from anything else, cyclotrons, the particle accelerators which generate the beams, cost millions.

In theory, these beams should be extremely accurate; in practice, 'There is some nervousness that what appears on the computer screen may not be happening in the patient,' Dr Camphausen fears.

Cryotherapy

Cryotherapy uses special instruments called cryoprobes to circulate extremely cold argon gas into the prostate and destroy cancer cells by freezing.

It's already been used to help with cancer that's recurred after radiotherapy, but it remains far from certain that it kills off all the cancer in the prostate. Also, the effects of cryotherapy on quality of life and long-term outlook are not yet clear. In clinical trials, side effects have included impotence in most recipients and incontinence in as many as one patient in every six. Other problems have been injury to the back passage and narrowing of the urethra.

'Men considering cryotherapy should understand that there are uncertainties about its effects,' advises NICE. 'There is not yet enough evidence on the long-term benefits.'

Unorthodox treatments

There are hundreds of 'natural', alternative, complementary and unconventional forms of treatment, including some like acupuncture and hypnotherapy which many oncologists and GPs find useful.

Acupuncture is increasingly provided these days in hospitals, hospices and clinics. Invented centuries ago in China, it uses fine needles which are painlessly placed just under the skin at various points on the body. For some people, this can help to relieve cancer pain, drug-related sickness, sleep disturbance and anxiety.

Hypnotherapy can help similarly. Patients are induced into a trance-like state where the body is deeply relaxed but the mind alert. It's not at all 'spooky', as some may fear – trance states are natural in daily life when daydreaming, for instance, or concentrating deeply on something to the exclusion of all else.

Most other remedies, ranging from herbs to oxygen to shark cartilage, lack scientific basis for their claims of effectiveness in treating or managing prostate cancer. There's no evidence from rigorous studies or clinical trials to support their use.

Such remedies may make a patient feel better yet have no positive physical effects on his prostate cancer. Some can cause serious side effects or interfere with effective conventional treatment. Indeed, some are nothing better than money-making scams. If the promised benefits sound too good to be true, they probably are.

Even so, mind can sometimes surprisingly triumph over matter. Just as some patients experience sudden remissions of even serious diseases, so have such treatments benefited some prostate cancer patients, albeit inexplicably. It could simply be down to the fact that alternative therapists often offer talk and time and a comforting personal touch, which can promote the more positive outlook which can so raise the spirits and enable improved mental health to perk up physical health.

Palliative care is not curative but is any treatment that improves the quality of a life towards its end, managing symptoms in the final stages of cancer to keep a man comfortable. It's often regarded, not only by the general public but even doctors, as suitable only when the disease has becomes terminal. However, NICE says that healthcare professionals should ensure that it's available not only then, not only towards the end of a life, but whenever it's needed.

Managing the symptoms of cancer pain, which is caused by tumours pressing on bones, nerves or other organs, can help patients considerably. Cancer pain can be very stressful and frightening but not everyone with a terminal illness will have it and it can be controlled without serious side effects

Other symptoms, notably feeling sick, breathing difficulties, tiredness, restlessness and confusion can be well-managed too. Care teams in palliative care wards or hospitals are skilled at allaying these and other problems. Many dying people find that gentle therapies such as massage and aromatherapy are very helpful or, if being touched hurts too much, meditation, visualisation or the Japanese technique, reiki, which uses 'laying on of hands' to promote healing.

Bisphosphonates, considered by the British Association of Urological Surgeons as a standard part of palliative treatment, can help to slow down the destruction of bone. Bone pain is common when prostate cancer has spread, typically after hormone therapy has stopped working.

Several bisphosphonates, such as ibandronate clodronate and zoledronic acid (brand name Zometa), are commonly prescribed to reduce pain, improve quality of life and possibly prolong survival by reducing the number of fractures and spine problems that men whose prostate cancer has spread to the bone may have. The chief side effects are tiredness, muscle aches, anaemia and, in a few cases, damage to bone tissue in the jaw.

Summing Up

- Treatment decisions hinge on many factors, which vary from man to man – the cancer's stage, the Gleason score, the patient's condition, thoughts and feelings.

- The patient himself should play a role in the way his prostate cancer is treated and never shrink from asking whatever questions he may have.

- The main medical treatments are active surveillance, surgery, radiotherapy, chemotherapy, hormone therapy and palliative care. Several new and potentially better therapies are being developed.

- All treatments have side effects. Although a few can sometimes be devastating, many are transient and most can be overcome or at least well-controlled.

- There is also a host of unorthodox, alternative treatments. Some can give real benefit but, unfortunately, far more lack any proper scientific basis and might even do harm.

Chapter Six

Life After Treatment

Longer survival

Everyone reacts to cancer treatment in their own way, both emotionally and physically. But 'prostate cancer is not a death sentence' is one of the first messages in this book and it deserves repeating. After all, if you've been treated for prostate cancer, the rest of your life is in front of you, and it may well be a long and gratifying one.

It's true that some 10,000 British men die annually from prostate cancer, usually after its spread to the lymph nodes, bones or other organs. But it's also true that far more men enjoy plenty of fulfilling years after treatment.

According to the latest research from Cancer Research UK's Cancer Survival Group, 60% of men in England with prostate cancer can expect to live for 10 years, three times longer than a generation ago. The reasons include quicker diagnosis, better surgery, smarter radiotherapy, improved techniques and new drugs.

Even so, treatment for prostate cancer can have various undesirable consequences, of which metastasis is just one. Many men will need to cope with at least some of them. This chapter considers how they can be managed and overcome.

Feelings

Prostate cancer and its treatment can alter how you feel about your family, your friends and, most of all, yourself. No two people react in the same way. There's no 'right' way, no 'wrong' way; it's what works best for you.

'There have been big increases in long-term survival, reflecting real progress in diagnosis and treatment.'

Professor Michel Coleman, Cancer Survival Group.

All sorts of concerns might arise, all sorts of feelings – shock, disbelief, confusion, numbness, bewilderment, worry, anger, depression, fear. Those feelings can wax and wane, come and go. They can be positive one day, sad the next.

It is only natural to be upset at times or to wonder what next, to be unsure about what to say to those closest to you, to work out how to hack it – you will do so, but in your own way. Just remember: you aren't alone. When you go for follow-up appointments, there'll be knowledgeable people to talk to and, perhaps even better, other men who are going through much the same experiences.

Support groups

Almost everyone with cancer needs support from someone else. There are all sorts of organisations which can give information and support (see Help List). Your doctor or specialist nurse can put you in touch with counsellors and other people skilled in helping people with cancer.

Particularly useful is being with other prostate cancer patients in a support group. There are scores in the UK. Some are for people with all forms of cancer, others are more specific; some are large, some for only a few. Their work and activities vary widely, ranging from social occasions to one-to-one counselling, but most give people ample opportunity to talk about their prostate cancer. That can be reassuring, heartening and thoroughly therapeutic.

'Once a week I get together with other men who've had prostate cancer treatment and the bonding that happens is brilliant,' says Bill Deakin, 62, who lives in Yorkshire. 'We each hear how other people are coping and that makes a real difference.'

Talking with others enables you to become really well informed about your condition and helps with ideas on how to cope with your feelings: a really good way to get through it all.

Also, don't hold back from quizzing your doctor about any aspect of your disease and care. For instance: what help can I get for dealing with my unpleasant symptoms and how I feel? How should I talk about my cancer with my partner, my children, other family members and friends? What practical help can I get? What about counselling? If you aren't happy with the answers to these and the many other questions you might have, say so. If you feel it's necessary, seek a second opinion. It's your right, and, after all, doctors can be wrong.

Above all, there's your family. Not all men want to talk about their feelings and problems, especially at first. Likewise, it can be hard for friends and relations to talk about your cancer, to share their thoughts or show their emotions. Before talking about things it's probably best to wait until you feel properly ready – but when you are ready, a good listener can help enormously.

Interestingly, a recent study of support groups in Canada showed that many important benefits result when women come to their meetings. By connecting with other women in the same boat and by sharing their experiences, they got more and better information, greater insight into the disease, greater reassurance and greater hope. Women's involvement is crucial, the study authors said – it adds value for both men and women to support groups.

Physical problems

Your feelings about yourself probably arise in large part from the physical changes that can follow prostate cancer and its treatment. Some of the effects you might experience could include:

- Tiredness.
- Pain.
- Incontinence.
- Sexual problems.
- Infertility.
- Side effects.

Tiredness

All forms of treatment have side effects and tiredness is a common one. Even the medicines used to treat the side effects can make you feel tired. You're likely to feel really drained for a time, especially right after treatment or if the prostate cancer is advanced.

A frequent cause is anaemia – when red blood cells don't carry enough oxygen from the lungs to the tissues. That can readily be dealt with by a blood transfusion or drugs. Other conditions, notably depression, a common after-effect of cancer diagnosis or treatment, may also cause fatigue, sometimes extreme – antidepressants can help with that.

Tiredness usually lessens over time but while it lasts you might, paradoxically, find it hard to go to sleep. Tell your doctor or cancer nurse if that's the case: there are several ways to counter it. People at support groups will probably be able to tell you how they've coped with sleep problems in the past too.

Surprisingly perhaps, one of the best answers to fatigue is exercise. It might seem silly to suggest this if you feel washed out, but it is the fact that light to moderate exercise, such as a short walk every day, does indeed help people with prostate cancer. A physiotherapist can give good advice on this.

Pain

Prostate cancer and its treatment usually mean that you will feel pain. It's also possible, of course, that the original prostate cancer will have been caught too late and therefore spread, to cause grief in the back, pelvis or elsewhere.

The degree of pain doesn't depend on the extent of the cancer. A large tumour can be painless; a small tumour can hurt like hell if it's pressing on nerves or has invaded bones. That's the cause of most cancer pain, but sometimes it's a result of treatment, for example, some drugs can cause numbness or tingling; radiation can irritate the skin.

The good news is that pain can almost always be relieved, so do tell your doctor or nurse if anything hurts. Don't imagine that awful pain is an inescapable part of having cancer: it isn't. The earlier you get it treated, the easier it will be to control.

Because pain differs from person to person, what works best depends not just on its cause but how it's tackled with an individual treatment plan. Give the doctor as much detail as you can. Say how often the pain occurs. Does it come on suddenly or gradually, and where? Is it a stabbing, aching or burning type of pain? Have you been able to do something about it yourself?

There can be pain after surgery or other treatments. Painkillers can work for many, but not in every case. However, there are lots of medications and powerful narcotics which can be used in various ways to provide the most accurate and appropriate pain control.

There are also answers to pain besides drugs. Surgery, radiation, nerve blocking and other special procedures such as acupuncture and hypnotherapy can help considerably, and a man himself can do a lot to help both mind and body, with help perhaps from his wife or partner, family or carers:

- Talk to someone about it.
- Or take your mind off it by listening to music, watching TV, reading or mental exercise (see chapter 7).
- Change your position regularly to prevent stiffness and sore skin.
- Use hot or cold packs.
- Breathe slowly and deeply to reduce tension.
- Get a relation or friend to gently massage your back, hands or feet.

Incontinence

Quite probably after surgery, radiotherapy or other treatments, the bladder will be affected.

Before treatment, when the prostate was enlarged, passing water might have been too slow to start, or perhaps there was dribbling. After treatment, many men lose control further, with poor flow or having to pee several times at night. Sometimes, bladder control goes completely.

Regrettably, both patients and doctors fight shy of discussing such difficulties, especially when they affect sex life as well. But in fact, there are many answers to them. Men should not, therefore, shrink from discussing them with the doctor or nurse. They might be referred to a specialist continence adviser. Incontinence pads these days are discreet and highly effective. Fortunately, few men get long-term or permanent incontinence.

Recovery can be helped with a balanced diet and drinking plenty of fluid, though not coffee, alcohol or too much tea.

Bowel problems – constipation or diarrhoea – can also occur, but are relatively easy to deal with. These too are often overlooked.

Sexual problems

Treatments for prostate cancer can have a variety of side effects which might affect your sex life.

As the prostate is such an important sexual organ, it's hardly surprising that during treatment and perhaps for some time after you might lose libido (sexual urge) and don't feel like sex at all. But some men feel quite the opposite and want to pack as much as possible into life.

Despite that, the tiredness which almost inevitably follows treatment can obviously be a 'turn off' for a while. That will probably pass.

More worrying for a third or even a half of men after treatment, is what doctors call 'erectile dysfunction': being unable to get or sustain an erection, especially after surgery, radiotherapy or hormone treatment. This will probably be temporary; however, after complete removal of the prostate or the testicles it's likely to be permanent. That can be very difficult to come to terms with.

Many men can't readily bring themselves to talk to their partner or doctor about such things. Many couples have seldom, if ever, talked frankly about sex. But if the outcomes of treatment or the fears it arouses 'bug' you or your partner, now is the time to discuss them, it really is.

Also, there are experienced counsellors and therapists who can help a lot. Quite often, you can be shown that it's anxiety which is the problem rather than truly physical impotence or treatment after-effects. And men today are lucky, for scientists have invented pills like Viagra, Cialis and Levitra, which can overcome impotence.

Whatever happens at first, remember that things could change. You'll need to wait until you feel more 'normal' to know how your sex life will be affected in the long run.

Infertility

Being unable to father a child can often result from prostate treatment (though not usually radiotherapy). As it's mostly older men who are affected, it won't be a cause for concern for many, but for men who hope to have children it can be awfully hard to accept. You should discuss it with your partner and the doctor, and before starting treatment look into the possibility of saving semen through sperm banking.

That said, the news isn't that bad. Even after chemotherapy, which is the main risk to fertility, three-quarters of men can still, after a time, father children unless the drug doses have had to be very high.

Surgical removal of cancerous lymph glands below the waist can also affect fertility. That's because the operation can cause semen to ejaculate back into the bladder rather than out through the penis. This happens only once in a hundred cases and it is not, in itself, harmful. But it can be upsetting. That's because no semen leaves the penis when a man has an orgasm and that renders him infertile. There's no cure for this unfortunate side-effect.

Effects of long-term treatment

Some side effects happen only after taking hormone treatment for a long time. They could include:

▧ Weight gain.

▧ Memory and sleep problems.

▧ Depression and/or mood swings.

▧ Osteoporosis.

▧ Increased risk of heart attack.

Weight gain

Some men on hormone treatment find it hard to keep their weight down. The causes of weight gain aren't clear but one might be that some men, understandably, feel less like exercising after treatment. Others perhaps find extra eating gives them a 'buzz' at a difficult time.

The best answer is a balanced diet and regular exercise (see chapter 7).

Memory problems and sleep disturbance

These plague some men who've had prostate cancer treatment, especially hormonal or other drugs. Medicine hasn't any snap solutions but reminder lists could help.

As with all post-treatment problems, the doctor or nurse should be told.

Depression and/or mood swings

Hormone therapy can strongly affect mood and all too often leaves patients feeling depressed. Talking to others – your wife, a relation or a trusted confidant – can best help you to see light at the end of the tunnel; others prefer a counsellor.

Osteoporosis

Osteoporosis is a thinning of the bones which can lead to fractures. It's a slightly higher risk for men on long-term treatment which blocks testosterone, the hormone which normally helps the constant process bone growth.

The condition can be treated with bisphosphonates such as alendronate (brand name Fosamax), extra vitamin D (best got from sunshine in the spring and summer) and calcium. The risks of osteoporosis can also be reduced by not smoking, strictly limiting alcohol, and regular exercise such as walking. Injectable bisphosphonates which promise to be much more effective are being developed.

'I'd burst into tears for no reason or was moody and cantankerous. The best help was talking to people I totally trusted. They made me think positive.'

Stephen, Norwich.

Increased risk of heart attack

After six months on hormone therapy, men older than 65-70 who already have heart disease are at greater risk of a heart attack. That's because some hormones' side effects, especially weight gain, can make heart disease worse.

Practical issues

Besides being faced with emotional and physical problems, you might well have practical issues to sort out like:

- Money matters.
- Support.
- Talking and listening.
- Talking to children.

That will take time. Try not to deal with everything at once – it will only magnify the difficulties. Doctors, specialist nurses, social workers, counsellors and a host of voluntary bodies can give invaluable help.

Money matters

You might be entitled to benefits, sick pay and even grants. There are many charities and professional bodies which can relieve financial distress for eligible people in need. Such organisations can sometimes give practical support to cancer patients and their families.

Going back to work is the best way not only to help with finances but to restore and boost morale. Otherwise, Macmillan Cancer Support, whose nurses provide free expert information and advice, is one of several bodies which can assist men with prostate cancer who are on low income and have few savings.

A healthcare professional has to refer you for a grant but financial help can be given to pay for home helps, childminders, home nursing, travel to and from hospital, heating, clothing, bedding, telephone installation and bills.

Social workers know about entitlement to sick pay and benefits. For men who live alone, they can help to organise recovery time after coming home from hospital.

For current or former members of the armed forces, there's a large network of ex-servicemen's organisations which can help.

Talking and listening

Deep, powerful feelings can well up when faced with cancer. Many men find it hard to talk about their prostate cancer and it's usually difficult for families too, because of the fear that the emotions will be too strong to handle.

Often, no one knows what to say or do even though they feel there must be something that would make things easier. The key message is: there's no 'right thing' to say; there's no ideal script. What matters most is not what we say but that we're there: someone's come to help, by talking, yes, but above all by being a good listener.

Laughter displaces gloom. Humour helps people deal with things that might otherwise seem impossible to cope with. Laughter boosts physical health by assisting good mood, promoting happier emotions. It actually triggers healthy physical changes, strengthening the immune system, for example. Laughter's an antidote to pain and stress and anger. It lightens burdens, inspires hope and helps you to be grounded.

'Being a good listener is the single most important thing you can do for a relative or friend,' says Macmillan Cancer Support. 'It can give them huge relief, even if you don't have all the answers. And there's nothing wrong with admitting "I don't know what to say".'

Good listening means not thinking about how to reply, not interrupting, not giving advice unless asked. It means encouraging the person to talk even if only by nodding or saying 'I see' or 'tell me more' without any questions. Or, even not saying anything – at times, long silences can 'say' a lot.

People often shy away from talking because they fear it might increase an existing anxiety. But psychologists say not talking is what makes anxiety worse. People with no one to talk to feel isolated and so are likelier to feel low.

Rather than going in at the deep end with 'Tell me about your feelings', a good way to start would be 'Do you feel like talking?'. If the answer's 'No', it might well be 'Yes' next time. Or vice versa – moods change.

The occasional question can be a useful opening, for example, 'Have you had any thoughts about . . .' or 'I've been thinking about . . . What about you?'

A partner might get asked 'what if?' questions. 'What if I can't pee?' 'What if I can't have sex?' 'What if I don't get better?' The answer might have to be, 'I'm not sure' or even 'I don't know' but that opens the way to exploring the issue, this might be comforting in itself.

'Am I a goner?' is a question that will certainly be in the mind, even if unspoken, of everyone with an advancing fatal disease. Many men will think about any 'unfinished business' whether this be personal, practical, financial or spiritual. Here again, a gentle question could help: 'Is there anyone you'd like me to get in touch with?', or a statement which asks a question: 'I guess you've been thinking a lot?'

Talking and listening will help a man to manage his fear and in time exorcise it, clear the mind of difficult, painful or oppressive feelings. Then, more at ease with himself, he can move on to living as full a life as possible.

Many people are afraid that negative thoughts or feelings might slow their recovery or make the cancer grow. That isn't so. It's very positive to recognise that at times, a man with cancer will feel angry, anxious, upset or sad.

The partner's role

The introduction to this book describes the prostate as a men-only organ. Indeed it is, but cancer of the prostate is far from being a men-only disease.

A partner is as much concerned about the cancer as the man they cherish. The role that a partner – wife, girlfriend, companion, or any close adult relation such as parent, son or daughter – can play in the management of their loved one's illness is crucial.

Partners need to know and understand what prostate cancer means not just for the affected man, but for them too.

'It's easy to feel there's no way out unless you have a partner or friend to keep you level and give you hope.'

Simon Flynn, Hunstanton.

A frequent worry that men may have after diagnosis and treatment is that the illness will damage the relationship. But what matters most, and what can contribute hugely to recovery, is that you work together to fight the cancer. Many who have been through this say their relationship has been strengthened and enhanced, bringing partners closer together than perhaps they have ever been. Each may find new values and a new meaning in life.

If you are the partner or close relative of someone affected by prostate cancer, you should:

- Offer time to talk and, if the offer isn't taken up, be patient – know that it depends entirely on up-and-down moods.

- Understand that patience is vital, though it's really hard to put into practice.

- Offer the chance to talk regularly.

- Receive the man's agreement or request to join him in the battle against the cancer and know how important it is to him that you are closely involved in all aspects of treatment and care.

- Know about everything that's happening.

- Ensure he accepts that you too might have personal issues to resolve.

- Have your own feelings and concerns heard.

- Be openly acknowledged for your help and care.

- Be told you're appreciated.

You should also:

- Recognise that you cannot be unaffected by the man's prostate cancer.

- Share your feelings and concerns with him openly and honestly.

- Be considerate, patient, supportive and caring.

- Know your limitations: you cannot 'fix' the cancer.

- Listen, talk and show your love and devotion.

- Attend medical appointments with the man but respect his wish for privacy should he request it.

- Accept that the person with cancer, no one else, is in charge of his care.

'I've never felt closer to my wife than I did after I was diagnosed.'
Canterbury patient.

Need2Know

Partner and patient together should:

- Inform themselves as fully as they can about the disease.
- Share feelings and not 'guess' what the other is thinking.
- Connect by talking.
- Be frank and open about sexual issues.

Talking to children

It can be really upsetting for a man to talk about his cancer with young children or grandchildren. But explaining the situation can help everyone involved to cope better.

Children readily sense when something's wrong and should be told the score simply and honestly. You don't need to explain everything, and indeed you shouldn't, but trying to shield them from the truth is counterproductive and can lead to all sorts of mistaken fears. Children are better at facing the truth than most adults appreciate. You can gently correct any misunderstandings.

There can be all kinds of reactions, from bad behaviour to fear, from guilt to stress-related illness, from deep distress to clinginess. But accept children as they are, show them you understand, instil feelings of hope. And reassure them that they are, and always will be, loved and cared for.

Recurrence

A recurrence is when cancer returns after a period, called a remission, when symptoms have lessened or disappeared. Even with the best treatment it can happen that a few cancer cells, either in the prostate or elsewhere in the body, are not detected, perhaps after lying dormant for some time and then starting to multiply again.

Recurrence can be:

- Local – in the same place or close to where it was first found and not spread.
- Regional – in the lymph nodes and tissue near the prostate.

'Get all the information you can so you are on the same wavelength as the doctor and can ask intelligent questions.'

Canterbury patient's wife.

- Distant – cancer has spread further away from the prostate.

If recurrence is some distance from the prostate, usually in one or more of the bones, the chances of cure are poor. This will cause pain, sometimes severe, especially in the lower back, as well as bone weakness (possibly causing fractures), fatigue and maybe fever and anaemia.

A recurrence brings back many of the old feelings and anxieties, including:

- Distress – the shock of finding that, despite treatment, the cancer hasn't gone can cause even more distress than before.

- Self-doubt – wondering if previous decisions and choices were the right ones.

- Anger – feeling bitter that cancer has returned, or perhaps rage with the doctors for not having stopped it.

Such feelings are understandable. It can help to think back to the first time and call on the same supports and ways of coping as before. Surprisingly perhaps, there are advantages this time:

- Knowing more about cancer, its treatment and what to expect can help reduce anxiety.

- The experienced patient can feel more in control and probably feels easier about talking frankly to the medics.

- Better understanding of the situation can help when making treatment decisions.

Summing Up

- The trend towards longer survival after cancer treatment is expected to continue. That's thanks to quicker diagnosis, better surgery, smarter radiotherapy, improved techniques and new drugs.

- Prostate cancer and its treatment arouse all sorts of feelings, positive and negative. They come and go, rise and fall. There are no 'right' or 'wrong' ways to feel: each individual must react in his own way.

- Almost everyone with cancer needs information and support. Partner, family, friends and many organisations can provide these.

- Tiredness, pain, incontinence and sexual problems are the most common physical effects of treatment. It's important to tell the doctor about any that occur because they can be managed and eased.

- There are also practical issues to sort out. They're best not tackled in a rush. Social workers, professional bodies and voluntary organisations can offer support in many ways.

- Men find it hard to talk about their prostate cancer. Often, no one knows what to say or do. What matters most is not what's said but that someone's there to be a good listener.

- Listening means being patient, gently encouraging the person to talk, not interrupting, not giving advice unless asked and not thinking about how to reply.

- If cancer returns after symptoms have lessened or gone, feelings of distress, self-doubt and anger might return. But the patient, being experienced, has better understanding of the situation and that can help when making treatment decisions.

Chapter Seven

Fitness After Treatment

After treatment, there's one obvious priority: to prevent cancer from returning or at least to minimise that risk.

Wives, partners, other relatives and friends can prepare meals, help with household chores, run errands, drive a man to the doctor or take him on a scenic run. People are often glad to lend a hand, it's a win-win situation: by helping the man with the cancer, they help themselves because it gives them a sense of making a contribution at a difficult time. Having prostate cancer affects the whole family and if friends and neighbours can help with meals or shopping or whatever else, that can do much to save the primary caregivers from burnout (psychological exhaustion).

However, after treatment, there might be problems with eating, which can be depressing. Loss of appetite can affect a man after prostate cancer treatment. Often, it's simply a case of feeling too tired or fed up to bother. Chemotherapy or radiotherapy can make the mouth sore and swallowing difficult.

Discuss any eating problems or changes in eating habits with a carer, especially a doctor, social worker or specialist nurse, who could refer to a dietitian.

There's one key thing about diet to bear in mind: although there are plenty of ways in which diet can help, and help significantly, there's no food or drink that can be guaranteed to prevent prostate cancer from developing or spreading.

Getting fit and keeping fit after treatment has three main elements:

- Balanced healthy diet.
- Regular sensible exercise.
- Keeping mentally active.

'We don't yet have evidence to say a change in diet could reduce the chances of prostate cancer from spreading.'
Professor John Toy, Cancer Research UK.

Balanced healthy diet

Balanced eating and drinking are crucial after every kind of prostate cancer treatment.

A balanced moderate-calorie diet:

- Keeps the immune system working well.

- Counters treatment side effects.

- Helps manage pain.

- Eases digestion.

- Counters constipation.

- Fights infections.

- Accelerates recovery.

- Encourages healing.

- Makes a man feel stronger and healthier.

All in all, a balanced diet, tweaked to suit personal tastes and medical concerns such as allergies, helps to ensure longer survival, especially if combined with sensible exercise and adequate rest.

Contents of a balanced diet

A good, balanced diet contains a variety of foods:

- Vegetables – plenty of raw or lightly cooked, cruciferous vegetables such as broccoli, sprouts, cauliflower and cabbage, which are nutrient-rich in fibre, vitamins and minerals. In broccoli especially, a chemical called 'sulforaphane' interacts with cells lacking the gene known as PTEN to lower the risk of prostate cancer recurring. Leafy greens such as spinach and kale are good too. The less cooked vegetables are, the more nutritional they are; ideally, they should be cooked in extra-virgin olive oil.

- Fruit – red grapes, strawberries, raspberries, watermelon and citrus fruits such as oranges, tangerines and satsumas. Also, pink grapefruit (unless you're taking statins to lower cholesterol or drugs for impotence).

- Antioxidants counteract free radicals, atoms or molecules which can start chain reactions and damage cells. Many experts say that the lycopene in cooked or sun-dried (but not raw) tomatoes, and even more in tomato juice, tomato sauce and tomato paste, can help to prevent prostate cancer. So might herbs. But the experts have differing views on this and it hasn't been shown for sure.

- Low-fat foods – some research suggests that food high in fat, such as red meat, cream and cheese, might provoke prostate cancer growth, but don't make your life a misery by utterly avoiding things you enjoy. Small portions in a moderate-calorie diet which is low in dairy produce and red meat might reduce the risk of renewed prostate cancer. If you like milk, use skimmed or semi-skimmed.

- Protein-rich foods such as skinned chicken and turkey, but not fatty poultry such as duck or goose, low-fat cuts of beef, pork, lamb, veal or lunch meats low in fat such as deli turkey, as well as eggs and lentils, are all good for men after prostate cancer treatment.

- Soy – traditional soybean products such as soy milk, tofu, misu, tempeh and soy sauce help to counter prostate cancer.

- Fish – nutritionists also recommend oily, coldwater fish such as salmon, mackerel, sardines and herring.

- Starchy foods – in addition, the experts speak highly of wholegrain (unrefined) bread, pasta and rice.

Superfoods (so-called) should be taken with 'a pinch of salt'. In recent years, dozens of ordinary groceries, ranging from beans and blueberries to turkey and yogurt, have been 'hyped' as if they were 'wonder drugs'. All, no doubt, are nutritious but claims that they can counter cancer are seriously overblown.

There were, for instance, manic headlines when researchers in California found that mice fed on walnuts developed prostate cancer tumours half the size of those in mice given their usual food.

The same sort of thing happened again when scientists at Southampton University found that certain chemicals in a single daily portion of fresh watercress could 'interfere' with cancer cell growth.

Cancer Research UK's health information manager Hazel Nunn put these and other reports into proper perspective. 'There's no reason,' she said, 'to believe that any one foodstuff would be superior to a generally healthy, balanced diet that is high in fibre, vegetables and fruit and low in red and processed meat, salt, saturated fat and alcohol.'

To be avoided

Salt should be left out of the diet as much as possible. There are two main reasons:

> **'No one foodstuff is superior to a generally healthy, balanced diet.'**
> Hazel Nunn, Cancer Research UK.

- Too much salt raises blood pressure and can do so dangerously. That can lead, and often does, to heart failure, kidney stones, stroke and, worst of all for men with prostate cancer, osteoporosis, often a major side effect of prostate cancer treatment (see chapter 6).

- Salt lurks in processed meats and luncheon meats, canned vegetables, soups, sauces and condiments, breakfast cereals, biscuits, bread, most snack foods such as crisps, as well as in butter, margarines and mayonnaise, fast foods and takeaways.

Sugar (including honey and malts) should also be avoided. Refined sugar, found in many kinds of processed foods from breakfast cereals to soft drinks, contains no fibre, minerals, proteins or enzymes. Devoid of all nutrients and providing only empty calories, it causes the body to deplete its own stores of vitamins and other essential organic substances.

The consequences can be dire. They include diabetes, gallstones and tooth decay. Sugar also thickens the blood, slowing its flow to the gums, causing gingivitis and gum disease.

If you feel like using food supplements, remember that they are just that, supplements not replacements. Far more beneficial sources of nutrition are fresh vegetables, fresh fruits and the other healthful foods listed above.

Muesli

Here's a tip for a wonderfully tasty and health-promoting breakfast: make your own muesli. Muesli was introduced 100 years ago in Switzerland for patients at a hospital where a diet rich in fresh fruit and vegetables was an essential part of therapy. Nowadays, supermarkets sell it in boxes just like cornflakes, but usually, and unnecessarily, they add sugar. Making your own takes five minutes for 2-4 days worth.

Ingredients

2 eating apples cored and grated

Juice of one lemon

3 tbsp of rolled oat flakes

2 tsp each seedless raisins, sesame seeds, pumpkin seeds, sunflower seeds, linseed, ground coconuts, pine kernels and flaked almonds or chopped hazelnuts

Method

- In a large bowl, mix grated apples with lemon juice, add the oats and rest of ingredients.
- Mix and add a little cold water to moisten, leave to soak.
- Eat with skimmed or semi-skimmed milk or yoghurt, or fruit juice if preferred.

Drink

Tap or bottled water is vital. It stands to reason – the body is 60-70% water. Blood is mostly water. Lungs and brain and muscles contain lots of water. Body temperature is regulated by water. Nutrients reach all vital organs thanks to water.

But after treatment for prostate cancer, especially if vomiting or diarrhoea have been side effects, dehydration can set in, with symptoms like joint or muscle pain, back pain, headaches, dizziness, constipation and sunken eyes. Plus the fact that, constantly, water is being lost through breathing, sweating and peeing.

The water in your body needs constantly topping up. You can calculate how much you need using the following rule: the number of fluid ounces equivalent to half the body weight in pounds, more or less. For example a person weighing 140lb would need 70fl.oz a day (around four pints). That's a lot, and if you exercise you'll need a bit more.

However, bear in mind that about a quarter of your water will come from fresh fruit and vegetables. Herbal tea and fruit juices, especially red grape juice and pomegranate juice, which might have anti-cancer properties, can provide more. But beware: sodas and sports drinks might contain sugar.

Red wine contains high levels of the chemical resveratrol, which may have some anti-cancer effects. But red wine contains many other chemicals too, one of them, potentially harmful, is alcohol itself. Even a couple of glasses can prompt incontinence.

A 2007 American research study suggested – suggested, not proved – that compared with beer or white wine, red wine might ward off prostate cancer, especially advanced or aggressive prostate cancer. But they didn't know why. 'It's far too early to endorse red wine for the prostate,' says chief researcher Dr Jane Stanford.

Exercise

Everyone knows that physical activity is good for health – mental as well as physical. Its benefits are particularly important after treatment for prostate cancer.

But working out or going for a walk are probably the last things that anyone will feel like doing after treatment. Having to cope with surgery, drugs or radiation can be tough in itself and then there are the physical problems discussed in chapter 6.

So, most men slow down after treatment. That's understandable, but it's not the right approach. To aid recovery, it's vital to exercise. Exercise is the best answer to post-treatment fatigue and feeling 'down'. It lessens the risk of the cancer recurring or spreading. It promotes longer survival because it improves what the experts call 'cardiovascular endurance' – greater ability of the heart, lungs and blood vessels to deliver to muscles and tissues the oxygen they need.

Exercise after prostate cancer treatment:

▓ Makes a man fitter, stronger and thinner.

▓ Boosts self-confidence and self-esteem.

▓ Increases motivation and feeling in control of one's life.

▓ Enhances body image.

▓ Lifts mood and lowers mild to moderate depression.

▓ Allays anxiety and stress.

▓ Distracts from worries.

▓ Combats frustration.

▓ Reduces cardiovascular disease and diabetes.

▓ Counteracts the bone thinning which often follows long-term hormone therapy.

▓ Moderates fatigue.

▓ Promotes deeper sleep.

By the way, this isn't about the strenuous workouts publicised by some 'celebrities' who've become gaunt and stringy through gross over-exercising. Exercise should be brisk and regular but moderate, never violent or painful; pleasant, never exhausting; well within a man's capacity and tailored to his overall condition.

'Exercise gives back to men who've been treated for prostate cancer a sense of control which has been diminished. It improves quality of life as a whole.'
Dr Nicole Culos-Reed, Calgary University, Canada.

Preparations for exercise

Exercising should start after a check-up and as soon as the doctor says it's okay. Discuss it with him or her, you could ask to be referred to an appropriate specialist for guidance.

- Get details of the exercises you could do which best meet your personal needs.

- Decide on goals. These can be challenging but must be achievable, not over-ambitious. They should be daily or weekly rather than long term. That way, you can feel yourself building on your successes.

- Start gently, progress gradually. Don't go wrong by doing too much at first - 10-15 minutes a day initially and not necessarily all at once. Build up from there to 30 minutes or more, as it suits you. Take a break every so often by missing out a day.

- Adopt activities that you'll enjoy; otherwise you'll dread doing them.

- Choose exercises that can be done throughout the year.

- Muscles take longer to get going in older age, so before exercising, stretch slowly and take time to warm-up, and afterwards to cool down.

- Wear clothes and footwear that are comfortable and suit the weather.

- If possible, exercise with someone else. That makes it more pleasant and helps you stick to a routine.

- Drink water every 15 minutes, especially when the weather's warm or humid. Drink even if you don't feel thirsty. That's because the sense of thirst tends to decline with age and isn't as good a guide to need as it used to be.

Exercises you could do

All-round, balanced fitness is best achieved by engaging in several forms of exercise.

Pelvic floor exercises, also known as Kegel exercises or pelvic muscle rehabilitation, are probably the most important exercises of all for men with any kind of prostate disorder.

Most men have problems of one sort or another with their urinary system. Leakage can be a real nuisance because of an enlarged or cancerous prostate. The problem is due to weakness in the pelvic floor – the network of muscles and other tissues which enable the pelvic organs, especially the bladder and urethra – to work properly and stop urine from leaking.

Exercises that strengthen the pelvic floor muscles will tighten, tone and regain control of the bladder (and, as a bonus, the bowel too). Done correctly, they will gradually improve or prevent leakage. Like any other muscles, the more they're used, the stronger they'll get.

Sit comfortably with thighs, buttocks and tummy muscles relaxed. Squeeze inside as if trying to hold back urine or wind. If you're not sure that you've identified the correct muscles, stop and then re-start a urine flow, but note – that's a test, not an exercise.

If you can't definitely feel a squeeze and some lift action of your pelvic floor, never mind – you'll still be able to learn the exercises, but will need to get professional advice.

Once the muscles begin to strengthen, you can exercise them while standing.

Hold drawing in and tightening as strongly and for as long as you can for up to 10 seconds. Then rest for 10-20 seconds: that's important. Then do the same again and if you can, hold longer and repeat for up to 12 long, strong holds. Then try 5-10 short strong ones.

Real improvement in pelvic floor muscle strength will take 3-6 months of this routine.

Don't:

* Hold your breath.

* Push down instead of squeeze.

* Pull the tummy in tightly.

* Tighten buttocks or thighs.

Walking is an excellent exercise for all-round recovery. Four or five short walks a day are better than one long walk. A flat, slow-moving treadmill does the same, but might be boring. If walking is tiring at first or makes you feel tired or sick, your body's telling you that you're doing too much. In a month or two though, you'll be up to pre-treatment strength and stamina.

Swimming is another valuable aerobic exercise. Regular swimming builds endurance, muscle strength and cardiovascular fitness. After other exercises, you can relax in the pool by just gently gliding through. Or simply float – then you can let your mind wander, a form of trance or meditation which can stimulate a feeling of wellbeing that leaves you relaxed, refreshed and upbeat.

Stretching – often overlooked, but for many the most enjoyable kind of exercise – makes muscles flexible, helps the joints move fully, avoids muscle soreness and tension, improves posture and, indeed, improves the physique generally.

It's best to stretch after a walk or other exercise, when the muscles are warm. Stretching cold muscles can cause injury. Don't bounce but hold each stretch for 15-30 seconds in a comfortable position until you feel a gentle pull on the muscle.

Yoga is a gentle, soothing exercise system, both physically and mentally. It's a combination of breathing exercises, physical postures, relaxation and meditation that's been practised for centuries. Yoga is ideal for people with health problems of all kinds, under a qualified practitioner, at first anyway, especially as some of the exercises aren't suitable for everyone. For more information see *Everyday Yoga – The Essential Guide* (Need2Know).

Other ways to exercise

Physical activity can be increased without joining a gym or even leaving the house. Just more activity in the daily routine can be valuable:

- Take the stairs instead of the lift.
- Walk up escalators.
- Park the car away from the house.
- Go for a bike ride.

- Walk rather than drive whenever practical.
- Take regular breaks to stand or stretch.

Exercise obsession

Too much exercise, and worse still an addiction to exercise, are as bad as none at all, harmful mentally as well as imprudent physically. To achieve fitness, it's crucial, especially after prostate cancer treatment, not only to rejuvenate the body but also let the muscles rest. What's more, compulsive exercising can cause burnout, making it far harder to stick to an exercise plan.

Mental exercises tone, protect and stimulate the brain, mind and spirit with endorphins, the body's own mood-elevating, pain-relieving compounds. Endorphins also reduce the amount of the stress hormone cortisol which the adrenal glands send into the bloodstream.

As with physical fitness, so with mental fitness: use it or lose it. The brain is plastic – it can change in response to learning. And just as there are physical exercises to improve and maintain physical health, so there are mental exercises to improve and maintain mental health.

Read as much as you enjoyably can. Take a sentence from a book or newspaper and try to make another sentence with the same words. You might find it useful to exercise your senses – for instance, do a smell and touch workout by trying to identify objects with eyes closed.

Crossword puzzles, anagrams and other games found in most newspapers, card games, board games, video games, are all good forms of mental exercise. Experts recommend the benefits not just of puzzles but of engaging in a variety of activities; the key is, don't get bored or stuck in a monotonous routine.

In short, stimulate the brain with interesting new tasks and tricks. Stay sharp, keep abreast of the world – if you vegetate mentally you'll stagnate physically.

Summing Up

■ After treatment, the obvious priority is to prevent cancer from returning or at least minimise that risk. Family, friends and neighbours can help you cope and recuperate.

■ A balanced, varied and calorie-moderate diet is crucial after any prostate cancer treatment, with plenty of fruit and vegetables and as low as possible in sugar and salt. Tap or bottled water in proportion to body weight is essential.

■ Exercise is particularly important after treatment for prostate cancer and has many benefits. It should be done only after medical advice and proper preparation and it shouldn't be overdone.

■ Pelvic floor exercises are probably the most important exercises of all for men with any kind of prostate disorder.

■ Stimulating the brain with interesting new tasks and tricks and by keeping abreast of the world is also important – if you don't stay sharp mentally, you'll stagnate physically.

Chapter 8

What Else can go Wrong with the Prostate?

Although the focus of this book is prostate cancer, the other prostate disorders must be considered when a man needs a diagnosis and the doctor plans treatment. In any case, it's possible to have prostate cancer and other prostate conditions at the same time. There is effective treatment and symptom relief for these 'benign' (non-cancerous) disorders of the prostate.

Benign prostate problems

There are two main ones:

▪ Prostatitis.

▪ Benign prostatic hyperplasia (BPH).

What are the symptoms?

Symptoms vary from man to man, but the main ones with all prostate problems (cancer included) are:

▪ Needing to urinate often, especially at night.

▪ Weak or interrupted flow.

▪ 'Jumpy' bladder – the urge to go comes more and more often.

▪ Straining to pee.

▪ Burning sensation when peeing.

- Taking a long time to finish peeing.

- Pain when urinating or during or after sex.

- Pain or discomfort in the penis, testicles, lower abdomen, lower back or when sitting.

- Blood in the urine.

- Disturbed sleep because of the need to pee.

- Involuntary leakage.

Often, there can be several such symptoms at once.

Prostatitis

Prostatitis is inflammation of the prostate which can occur at almost any age. Besides swelling or pain, it can also lead to feelings of tiredness, depression and can cause sexual problems.

Apart from prostate cancer itself and BPH, detailed later in this chapter, prostatitis is far from understood and there is no widely accepted cause. A major one is probably acute infection caused by bacteria, a virus or a sexually transmitted disease. Sometimes, an immune system disorder might be responsible. Stress and infrequent sexual activity can also underlie prostatitis.

Does the cause matter?

Yes, because it should help to find a cure. But determining the cause is far from easy. Urologists differ sharply about what does, or might, cause prostatitis. Even doctors who are sure of the cause cannot always cure it, and antibiotics often don't work or have unpleasant side effects.

Unfortunately, checking for infection by a hard-pressed doctor can be too hurried – do insist on a careful check. But even if bacteria are found, that can't always help to cure the condition. Considering another cause might not help either.

What else might help?

Relaxation techniques, or strengthening the pelvic muscles (see chapter 7), can help. Other treatments include anti-inflammatory drugs, muscle relaxants, hot baths, drinking plenty of water and frequent ejaculation.

Take charge!

But no one approach works for everyone. This often means that you, the patient, should take charge. Be well-armed with questions, demanding of your doctor and decide what works best for you.

BPH

Although the prostate enlarges undesirably with BPH, the condition isn't cancer. Nor does it make cancer more likely.

Prostate cancer invades tissue by growing outward from its starting point on the outer layer of the gland. BPH starts deeper down and grows inward, ever more tightly squeezing the urethra.

The symptoms – urinary hesitancy, frequent urination, painful urination, urinary tract infections, urine retention – sooner or later become all too evident. By contrast, prostate cancer is often without symptoms for years.

Most men will develop an enlarged prostate if they live long enough. The risk increases every year after age 40 or so, so that by age 70, three quarters of all men will have it. Of these, some 25% will need treatment, sometimes more than once, to relieve the urine blockage that BPH causes.

What causes BPH?

The quick answer is, we don't know. Like wrinkles and grey hair, BPH just seems to come with age, from around age 40 onwards.

But there are plenty of suggestions – one reason might be that BPH sets two types of tissue in the prostate at odds. On the one hand, there are epithelial cells. These make the prostate's secretions. On the other hand, there are smooth muscle cells. These eject those secretions into the urethra. Epithelial tissue helps to form nodules which can interfere with the flow of urine from the bladder. Then, smooth muscle tissue reacts by tightening around the urethra.

A second theory is that the prostate becomes more sensitive to changes in the balance between the sex hormones in middle-aged and elderly men. Gradually increasing levels of male hormones from puberty onwards, especially testosterone, the main one, are almost certainly part of the cause.

Yet another idea is that BPH might be triggered by 'growth factors' – naturally occurring substances which regulate cellular processes in the prostate.

Perhaps the most intriguing fact is that in men with BPH, growth in the prostate is not cancerous, not due to more cells being made (as with cancer) but due to existing cells living longer. Some experts suggest that understanding what controls the life and death of cells in BPH could point the way to controlling them in cancer too.

Does BPH run in some families?

Some studies suggest that it does. A few men inherit one or more genes that seem to make them prone to BPH. In one study of men with significant prostate enlargement, male relatives were four times as likely as other men to have BPH and their brothers were six times as likely.

Some 'nots' about BPH

- BPH does not make it more likely that you will develop prostate cancer.
- Even if there are urinary tract symptoms, BPH does not diminish the need to drink plenty of fluid. In fact, it increases that need because it prevents infection caused by insufficient urine flow.
- BPH is not life-threatening but that does not mean that a man has to put up with its undesirable symptoms. They can be treated.

- A bigger prostate resulting from BPH does not cause you to pee more often because urine production is not the role of the prostate, but the kidneys.

- BPH does not cause infertility and does not necessarily lead to incontinence.

- Surgery for BPH does not necessarily affect the desire for sex but might affect sexual function.

Treatments for BPH

- Doing nothing.
- Surgery.
- Drugs.
- Other treatments.

Doing nothing

Before the 1990s, surgery was the only effective treatment. Things are better now. Modern drugs can be effective in many (though not all) cases. They can, of course, have unwanted side effects.

'If the symptoms are not too bad,' says urologist Professor David Kirk, 'Most men just need reassurance that their condition isn't dangerous and advice about simple measures, such as being sensible about the amount they drink and taking enough time to empty their bladder. They can learn to live with what may be only minor symptoms.'

Surgery

If the symptoms are mild, surgery for BPH will probably not help a lot. But when, as with retention, they're severe, an operation is the best answer. It's safe unless a man is frail or very unfit.

If the prostate is very overgrown, the favoured method is still traditional open surgery, with the enlarged part cut out. A more usual procedure nowadays is 'keyhole' surgery called transurethral resection of the prostate – TURP.

An instrument called a resectoscope is inserted, after local anaesthetic, through the urethra. The surgeon can see what needs to be done and uses the instrument to remove the offending tissue. It takes about half an hour. Urine drains away through a catheter for a couple of days.

Drugs

There are two types of drugs for BPH. They're usually prescribed if symptoms are mild or if surgery is unsuitable.

- Alpha-blockers are tablets or capsules which relax muscles within the prostate, reducing obstruction and increasing urine flow. Among them are prazosin (brand name Hypovase), indoramin (Doralese), tamsulosin (Flomax) and terazosin (Hytrin). Side effects vary, so if one isn't suitable, another can be tried. The chief advantage is that they work immediately (though not for everyone). The chief disadvantage of some is that they act on other muscles, causing weakness, lethargy and dizziness.

- One tablet daily of hormonal agents such as finasteride (Proscar) and dutasteride (Avodart). These block the action of testosterone, shrinking the prostate by up to a third and reducing PSA level. Sexual difficulties in a minority are the main unwanted effects. If hormones aren't taken indefinitely, prostate growth will return. Also, finasteride can misleadingly lower the PSA count, which could lead to a dangerous false-negative result.

Other treatments

- Heating the prostate with a probe inserted through the urethra or into the back passage can improve symptoms, but only in milder cases.

- Lasers can be used to remove prostate cell enlargements but urologists don't agree on how they're best used or even if they should be used at all.

- Stents, small metal tubes put in the prostate to open it, were widely used until recently but led to long-term problems. They're now recommended only in special circumstances.

- Herbs – so-called 'natural' remedies – can be bought over the counter at pharmacies and health food shops. Although they might work for some men, there's no clear evidence that they work for everyone. They're probably harmless, but it's best to check with the doctor before taking them. Like finasteride, they might harmfully affect the PSA count.

Summing Up

- When there's a prostate problem and diagnosis is needed, prostate disorders other than cancer must be considered.

- The two main non-cancerous prostate disorders are prostatitis (inflammation) and BPH. Although the symptoms are like those of prostate cancer itself, they aren't life-threatening and they can't spread beyond the prostate.

- There are several effective treatments and forms of symptom relief for both prostatitis and BPH. But when symptoms are tolerable, as they often are, they're probably best left without medical intervention.

- No one approach works for everyone. The patient should decide what's best for him personally. He should be demanding of the doctor and not hold back from asking whatever questions he has.

Chapter 9

Research and Future Prospects

Understanding prostate cancer

American research teams in Michigan and New York have identified at least 24 different types of prostate cancer.

Could anything show better how complex a disease prostate cancer is, and so difficult to understand?

It's merely one example of the hundreds of ways in which, month after month, new developments in understanding and treating prostate cancer emerge.

And with every scientific breakthrough, with each medical innovation, there are fresh questions for scientists to answer.

This chapter outlines just some of the many prostate cancer research projects now under way.

'The reality is there is no real, lasting cure for prostate cancer.'
Professor Sir Bruce Ponder.

Words of warning

It is true, as Dr. Tom Stuttaford has said, that the past two decades have seen dramatic improvements in the prospects for prostate cancer treatment.

But for all the new trials and discoveries, the true nature of prostate cancer is still in doubt. Its cause or causes are unknown. Some are suspected but none is proven. Ways to prevent it are elusive. Drugs used to treat it are imperfect.

There is no real or lasting 'cure', no 'magic bullet' to conquer prostate cancer, or any cancer, according to Professor Sir Bruce Ponder, director of the Cancer Research UK's Cambridge Research Institute.

Optimistic outlook

Despite that, he told the BBC, 'There's a new sense of optimism in research.'

Half of the investigators at the Institute are in basic research – trying to understand how malignancies such as prostate cancer develop.

Others are looking at new methods of imaging, analysis and investigation. 'Recent advances have made our understanding of cancer ready for application in the clinic,' Prof. Ponder says.

'Our aim is research that benefits patients directly, that reduces the number who die of cancer and that improves their quality of life.'

More words of warning

And there are indeed a lot of hopeful and impressive findings in the research projects outlined here.

Yet, science needs to be sceptical and is always provisional. No theory can be accepted at face value; every result needs to be independently tested and re-tested.

That's in the nature of research. Nobel prize-winner Richard Feynman put it well: 'In no field is all the research done. Research leads to new questions to answer by . . . more research.'

Genetic research

Cancer experts believe that more answers to prostate cancer will come from the 25-30,000 blueprints of the body's structure, the genes, than from anywhere else.

However, leading geneticist Professor Steve Jones, of University College, London, thinks otherwise. 'It's plain wrong to think that a few genes hold the key to ridding the world of prostate cancer,' he insists. 'Hundreds of genes are probably responsible and are perhaps less important than diet, lifestyle and the environment.'

Meanwhile, though, investigators are focusing on how genetic engineering might help to overcome it. But, warns Wellcome Trust director Sir Mark Walport, 'Cancer is complicated. We must balance the hype and the hope.'

- The UK Genetic Prostate Cancer Study (UKGPCS) is looking into how family history can increase a man's risk of prostate cancer.

- Researchers hope to learn how many families have a strong history of the disease and how great the risk is for men in such families. They also aim to identify all faulty genes that can increase prostate cancer risk. Maybe, in time, diagnosis could be much earlier than now.

- The latest gene analyses shows that a half of prostate tumours grow slowly and are not highly malignant. Around 10-12% of men have the fastest-growing tumours. Another 10% develop prostate cancers which are less menacing but still threatening enough to need treatment. Genetic tests could lead to shorter and gentler treatment with fewer unpleasant side effects.

- Cambridge scientists are searching for 'genetic cards' that determine an individual's risk of cancer. They suggest that the chance of a man getting prostate cancer is like being dealt a hand of cards. His risk depends on whether or not he inherits good cards and on how he plays them – his lifestyle.

- Some genes carry a very high risk, which is why some men have a strong family history of cancer. More often, a combination of genes confers a moderate risk.

- Men whose index finger is longer than their ring finger might be a third less likely develop prostate cancer. Finger length is fixed in the womb and is thought to relate to levels of the sex hormone testosterone. Lower exposure to it results in a longer index finger. But as more than half of all men have shorter index fingers, they needn't worry.

Possible new treatments

An experimental vaccine called Provenge spurs the immune system into fighting advanced prostate cancer that does not respond to anti-androgen treatment.

Unlike other vaccines, for measles or chickenpox say, which are applied before a person is ill; Provenge would be given after the cancer had been diagnosed.

The clinical benefits of hyperbaric (high pressure) oxygen therapy (HOT) in patients who still have serious gastrointestinal side effects a year after standard radiotherapy are being researched in Britain.

HOT has long been used to treat scuba divers for the bends and sportsmen for quick healing of injuries. It works by delivering bursts of oxygen to stimulate the protein which controls cell growth and repair.

A natural prostate fluid called citrate might detect prostate cancer in only three minutes by measuring the wavelength of light when it's shone through it. That could reduce or even remove the need for prostate biopsies.

'I was in severe pain with prostate cancer which had spread to my bones. Chemotherapy and other treatments had failed. But abiraterone has given me a year so far of near normality'
Simon Bush, 50 London bank manager.

Potential new drugs

A new drug called abiraterone offers a more thorough blockade of testosterone than any current anti-androgens and might come into use soon.

It works by blocking not only the hormones in the testes, chiefly testosterone, that drive the growth of prostate cancer tumours, but also elsewhere in the body, including the cancer itself.

In trials, men with prostate cancer who continued with abiraterone for as long as two years or more were able to control the disease with 'manageable' side-effects. Several could stop taking morphine to relieve bone pain

Until now, a prostate cancer and growths from it which have become hormone-refractory gave most patients only about 18 months of good quality of life. 'Abiraterone throws 75% of them a lifeline of hope.' says Dr. Tom Stuttaford.

A trial to find a treatment better than hormone therapy for prostate cancer has been started by British researchers. In trials, hundreds of men are being given hormones or are having orchidectomies (testicles removal).

Then, to see which treatment is best, some will also get the cancer-blocking drug docetaxel, or the bisphosphonate zoledronic acid (brand name Zometa), or celecoxib, a drug that's also very effective against arthritis pain, or various combinations of these drugs.

Researchers have found that men who take a low daily dose of aspirin are a third less likely to be diagnosed with prostate cancer than those who did not. No other painkilling anti-inflammatory drugs, such as ibuprofen, had the same effect. On the other hand, regular aspirin could have serious side effects.

More potential medications

- The anti-diabetes drug rosiglitazone and cholesterol-lowering fenofibrate might control prostate cancer by stabilising or lowering PSA in the blood, British researchers say. Neither drug has such severe side effects as chemotherapy. Although rosiglitazone treats diabetes, it's still safe for men who aren't diabetic.

- Can the anti-impotence drug Cialis help with sexual function after prostate cancer surgery? A trial to see if its early use can achieve this is recruiting volunteers in Cambridge, London and Middlesbrough.

- Two radioactive drugs called cholines might help to show up prostate cancer which has spread to other parts of the body. Researchers led by Dr. Michael O'Doherty, a consultant in nuclear medicine at Guy's and St Thomas' NHS Trust, London, are assessing their value. The drugs would be used in PET scans combined with CT scans.

- A trial comparing oestrogen patches stuck on the skin with hormone injections for prostate cancer is being conducted by researchers. Urologist Professor Paul Abel of Imperial College, London, believes the patches will work as well as the jabs but will cause fewer side effects. The main concern is that they might affect the heart.

Other investigations

- Men in their 50s who had sex more than ten times a month got some protection against prostate cancer, according to a study at Nottingham University

- Men in their 20s who ejaculate every day are a third less likely to develop prostate cancer later in life because cancer-causing chemicals in fluid from the prostate build up in the gland over time, and daily masturbation could flush them out.

- Infertile men are at higher risk of developing rapidly growing, rapidly spreading prostate cancer because unknown biological pathways might be at work, investigators say. When 4,500 infertile men were studied, they were more than twice as likely to be diagnosed with high-grade prostate cancer than men who weren't infertile.

- Socialising is better than surgery, drugs or radiotherapy at causing prostate tumours to shrink or even disappear, according to recent research. 'Doctors should pay more attention to the living conditions of their patients,' asserts Ohio neuroscientist Professor Matthew During. 'Living in an environment rich with physical, mental and social stimulation appears by itself to curb cancer growth even if, or even because, it's mildly stressful.' he believes.

- Men are more likely to develop prostate cancer if they're subject to typically British cold weather and lack of sun. American scientists point out that there's more prostate cancer in northern countries than further south, perhaps because cold weather slows the breakdown of cancer-inducing industrial pollutants and pesticides in the atmosphere. Also, too little sun could increase prostate cancer risk through vitamin D deficiency.

- The side effects of radiotherapy, such as impotence and incontinence, and the total radiation given could be reduced by placing a small balloon next to the prostate before treatment. The balloon, now on trial, is filled with saline solution until it's about the size of a peach. It's then implanted under local anaesthetic so that it pushes healthy tissue away from the radiation beams. The balloon dissolves in 3-6 months, the usual duration of prostate cancer radiotherapy.

Need2Know

- A urine test for PSA3, under development and not available on the NHS, could detect prostate cancer more reliably than standard tests for PCA in the blood, researchers say. In the long run, this might reduce or even remove the need for biopsies, according to urologist Dr. Christopher Amling. The PCA3 urine marker is specific for prostate cancer. It determines whether the products of genes associated with prostate cancer are in the urine. Unlike the standard PSA test, the test for PSA3 isn't affected by the size of the prostate or by non-cancerous prostate conditions such as BPH. It's also less affected by urinary infections, which can make the PSA test completely unreliable.

Future research needs

There's a real need for cancer doctors to distinguish between men who will die *from* the prostate cancer and those who will die *with* it, says the National Institute for Health and Clinical Excellence (NICE).

Research into this is vital because doctors need to clear up doubts about which cancers are clinically important, which treatments to choose and when to use them.

NICE notes that prostate cancer diagnoses have improved so much that many are made nowadays in men who don't even have symptoms. That makes it essential to know who are likely to benefit from full-on treatment.

NICE calls for research into the value of treatments which aim to wipe out localised prostate cancer in its first stage, when it is advanced locally and when it's recurrent locally.

This means that such procedures as brachytherapy, cryotherapy, high intensity focused ultrasound and others must be 'rigorously examined' to show how much they improve survival and quality of life, and what the side effects are.

Summing Up

- Prostate cancer is such a complex disease that hundreds of scientists in hundreds of laboratories are working to understand it.

- They say there is no cure but are still optimistic about finding new ways to manage, combat and outwit the disease.

- Experts believe that more answers to prostate cancer will come from genetic research than from anything else.

- Many new drug treatments are being devised and developed, especially in the UK and the US.

- Researchers have also shown that a man's sex life and other personal characteristics can be a major influence on his risk of developing prostate cancer.

- Research breeds research. There are always new questions to answer. Perhaps the most important is: what distinguishes men who will die *from* prostate cancer and those who will die *with* it.

Help List

There are innumerable sources of information, help, support and advice about prostate cancer – so many that it could be confusing. The Internet has literally thousands of websites on prostate cancer but most of them, for one reason or another, could waste your time, and your patience! Below are details of the best of them and there should be no need to look up any others.

British Acupuncture Council

63 Jeddo Road, London, W12 9HQ
Tel: 020 8735 0400
www.acupuncture.org.uk
The British Acupuncture Council is a self-regulatory body for the practice of traditional acupuncture in the UK, establishing and maintaining high professional standards, funding clinical research and works with the Department of Health towards statutory regulation of acupuncture.

British Association for Counselling and Psychotherapy

15 St John's Business Park, Lutterworth, Leicestershire, LE17 4HB
Tel: 01455 883316
bacp@bacp.co.uk
www.bacp.co.uk
The BACP's helpdesk enables people to find a suitable counsellor in their area with whom they will feel comfortable. It seeks to remove any anxieties that might be associated with choosing a counsellor and are glad to discuss any queries or concerns which may arise when choosing a counsellor or during counselling.

British Society of Clinical Hypnosis

Tel: 01262 403103
sec@bsch.org.uk
www.bsch.org.uk
The British Society of Clinical Hypnosis is a national professional body whose aim is to promote and assure high standards in the practice of hypnotherapy. Registration demands good quality training, ethical practice and adherence to its code of conduct.

Cancer Research UK

P.O. Box 123, London, WC2A 3PX
Tel: 020 7242 0200
www.cancerresearchuk.org
Cancer Research UK's website is probably the most comprehensive and easily understood of all, providing clear information on every possible aspect of prostate cancer. Cancer Research UK aims to save lives by providing information, by supporting research by thousands of scientists, doctors and nurses and by influencing public policy. It is the European leader in the development of new anti-cancer drugs and the world's largest cancer research organisation outside the US.

Everyman

The Institute of Cancer Research, Freepost LON 922, London, SW7 3YY
Tel: 0800 731 9468
everyman@icr.ac.uk
www.everyman-campaign.org
Everyman was established by The Institute of Cancer Research, the research department of the Royal Marsden Hospital, London, to raise awareness and fund research for prostate (and testicular) cancer. Money raised supports the UK's first centre dedicated to diagnosis, prevention and treatment.

Health Talk Online

www.healthtalkonline.org
This prize-winning website enables viewers and listeners to share other people's experiences of health and illness as well as to find reliable information validated by specialists at Oxford University. There are 55 interviews of men who have experienced prostate cancer.

Macmillan Cancer Support

Head Office, 89 Albert Embankment, London, SE1 7UQ
Tel: 0808 808 0000 (helpline)
cancerline@macmillan.org.uk
www.macmillan.org.uk
Macmillan Cancer Support provides care and support for people with cancer at every stage of their illness through Macmillan nurses, Macmillan doctors and a programme of financial help for patients in need. It offers information, advice and emotional support to cancer patients and their families. It has publications about the main types of cancer, treatments and ways of living with cancer. The free-phone helpline and letter information service has a team of specialist cancer nurses able to advise on all aspects of cancer and treatment. A benefits line offers advice on financial matters.

National Institute for Health and Clinical Excellence (NICE)

MidCity Place, 71 High Holborn, London, WC1V 6NA
Tel: 0845 003 7780
nice@nice.org.uk
www.nice.org.uk
The National Institute for Health and Clinical Excellence provides guidance, sets quality standards and manages a national database to improve health and prevent and treat ill health. It contains a wealth of information on prostate cancer but, aimed chiefly at health professionals, this might prove overwhelming with detail and the curse of 'too much information'.

Penny Brohn Cancer Care

Chapel Pill Lane, Bristol, BS20 0HH
Tel: 0845 123 23 10 (helpline)
helpline@pennybrohn.org
www.bristolcancerhelp.org
Penny Brohn Cancer Care is Britain's leading holistic cancer charity that
has taken forward the Bristol Approach to complementary cancer care. This
Approach works with medical treatment plus a unique combination of physical,
emotional and spiritual support using complementary therapies and self-help
techniques, including practical advice on nutrition.

Prostate Brachytherapy Advisory Group

www.prostatebrachytherapyinfo.net
The Prostate Brachytherapy Advisory Group takes an active interest in the
commissioning of services and the provision of high-quality, low-dose rate,
permanent seed implant prostate brachytherapy. Its website gives full information
on the technique and its website lists brachytherapy centres in the UK.

The Prostate Cancer Charity

First Floor, Cambridge House, 100 Cambridge Grove, London, W6 0LE
Tel: 0800 074 8383 (helpline)
info@prostate-cancer.org.uk
www.prostate-cancer.org.uk
The Prostate Cancer Charity works to improve the care and welfare of people
whose lives are affected by prostate cancer through research, support,
information and campaigning.

Prostate Cancer Support Association

Tel: 0845 601 0766 (helpline)
helpline@prostatecancersupport.info
www.prostatecancersupport.co.uk
The Prostate Cancer Support Association is a national body of self-help and
support groups. It lists about 60 throughout England and Wales.

Prostate UK

www.prostateuk.org
This website provides patients, carers and the general public with detailed information about prostatic diseases. It also funds research into their prevention, treatment and management as well as training for healthcare professionals.

Tenovus

43 The Parade, Cardiff, CF24 3AB
Tel: 0808 808 1010 (helpline)
www.tenovus.com
Tenovus is a charitable organisation seeking control of cancer through quality research, prevention, education, counselling and patient care. Tenovus also funds support and counselling services for cancer patients and their families through teams of nurses, counsellors and social workers.

UK Prostate Link

www.prostate-link.org.uk
UK Prostate Link is an exceptionally useful portal website that leads to the best quality Internet information about prostate cancer. It monitors the top websites for up-to-date information, assesses its quality and has an easy-to-search database.

Glossary

Active surveillance
Managing low or intermediate-risk localised prostate cancer, allowing radical treatment to be targeted only at those who would benefit most.

Adenocarcinoma
Most prostate cancers are adenocarcinomas – malignant cells from the prostate's lining.

Aggressive
Cancer that grows or spreads quickly.

Androgens
Hormones that promote male sex characteristics.

Benign
A growth that is not cancerous.

Benign prostatic hyperplasia (or hypertrophy) (BPH)
A non-cancerous condition in which an overgrowth of prostate tissue pushes against the urethra and the bladder, blocking the flow of urine.

Biopsy
Removal of small samples of body tissue for microscopic examination to assist diagnosis.

Bone scan
Imaging to show any abnormal areas of bone.

Brachytherapy
A form of radiotherapy in which radioactive pellets or wires are put into the prostate.

Carcinogen
A substance which can cause cancer.

Catheter
A hollow tube used to drain fluids from or inject fluids into the body.

Chromosome
Thread-like strands in body cells which contain genes.

Computerised tomography (CT)
An X-ray of the body's organs that spots abnormalities.

Cryotherapy
Freezing the prostate to eradicate prostate cancer.

Cystoscopy
Looking directly into the bladder or urethra through a cystoscope.

Digital rectal examination (DRE)
Putting a lubricated gloved finger in the back passage to feel the prostate for any abnormalities.

Dysuria
Painful or difficult urination.

Ejaculation
The release of semen through the penis.

Erectile dysfunction (impotence)
Consistent inability to get or sustain an erection.

External beam radiotherapy
High energy radiation beams focused on cancer cells to kill them.

Gene
The basic unit in every cell of the body which carries the information that determines characteristics inherited from parents.

Gland
An organ that makes one or more substances, such as hormones, digestive juices, sweat, tears or saliva.

Gleason score
The system for grading the seriousness of a man's prostate cancer.

Grade
The degree of malignancy of a tumour, judged by its appearance under the microscope.

Haematospermia
Blood in the semen (not in the sperm, despite its medical name).

Haematuria
Blood in the urine.

High intensity focused ultrasound (HIFU)
High frequency sound waves aimed at the cancer and heating the cells to eradicate the cancer.

Hormones
Chemicals produced chiefly by the endocrine glands that help to regulate growth and development.

Hyperplasia
An abnormal increase in the number of cells in an organ or tissue.

Hypertrophy
Enlargement or overgrowth of an organ in whole or part due to an increase in size of its constituent cells.

Impotence
Consistent inability to get or sustain an erection.

Incontinence
Loss of bladder and bowel control.

Libido
Sexual urge.

Locally advanced prostate cancer
Cancer which has broken through the covering of the prostate, often to nearby organs such as the back passage or bladder.

Local treatment
Treatment that is directed at tumour cells in one localised area.

Localised prostate cancer
Cancer confined to the prostate gland.

Lymph
Clear fluid that carries cells which help fight infections and other diseases.

Lymph nodes
Small bean-shaped glands throughout the body that filter lymph fluid, important for proper working of the immune system.

Lymphatic system
The tissues and organs that produce, store and carry white blood cells to fight infections and other diseases.

Malignant
Cancerous.

Magnetic resonance imaging (MRI)
A non-invasive method of imaging (not an X-ray) which shows up tissues and organs.

Meatus
The opening of the urethra at the end of the penis.

Medical castration
Hormonal therapy to reduce levels of testosterone hormone made by the testicles.

Metastasis/metastatic
Spread of cancer to other organs or tissues through the blood or lymphatic system.

Metastatic prostate cancer
Cancer which has spread from the primary site in the prostate to the lymph nodes or other parts of the body.

Oncologist
A doctor who specialises in treating cancer.

Orchidectomy
Removal of both testicles to reduce the level of testosterone (also called surgical castration).

Osteoporosis
Loss of bony tissue which makes bones brittle and liable to fracture.

Palliative
Treatment which does not cure but improves symptoms and quality of life.

Perineum
Area just behind the scrotum in front of the anus.

Placebo
An inactive dummy used in drug trials to show how effective the active drug is.

Positron emission tomography (PET)
Imaging with a radioactive tracer to produce a computerised image which helps diagnose cancer, see how far it has spread and check response to treatment.

Prognosis
The medical view of the likely course or outcome of a disease or condition.

Prostatectomy
Surgery to remove part or all of the prostate gland.

Prostate Specific Antigen (PSA)
Protein secreted by the prostate and used to help detect and follow prostate cancer.

Radiotherapy
The use of radiation, usually X-rays or gamma rays, to kill tumour cells.

Rectum
Back passage: the last several inches of the large intestine that ends at the anus.

Resorption
Bone growth.

Retention
Being unable to pee.

Retropubic prostatectomy
Removal of the prostate through a cut in the abdomen.

Scrotum
The bag of skin that contains the testicles and helps to regulate their temperature.

Semen
The thick white fluid containing sperm that a man ejaculates.

Sperm
The male seed that can fertilise the female egg to make babies.

Surgical castration
Removal of the testicles (orchidectomy) to lower the level of testosterone.

Testes/Testicles
The two glands ('balls') inside the scrotum which produce sperm, testosterone and other sex hormones.

Testosterone
The major male hormone.

Trans-urethral resection of the prostate (TURP)
Keyhole surgery to remove tissue from the prostate using a resectoscope put into the urethra.

Transrectal ultrasound scan (TRUS)
An examination of the inside of the prostate using high frequency sound waves.

Tumour
Abnormal tissue growth (not necessarily cancer).

Ultrasound
High-energy sound waves which are bounced off internal tissues or organs to make echoes which form a sonogram, a picture of them.

Urethra
The tube leading from the bladder through which urine leaves the body.

Urology
The branch of medicine concerned with diseases of the urinary organs and reproductive systems.

Vasectomy
Minor operation to make a man infertile.

Need - 2 - Know

Available Titles Include ...

Allergies A Parent's Guide
ISBN 978-1-86144-064-8 £8.99

Autism A Parent's Guide
ISBN 978-1-86144-069-3 £8.99

Blood Pressure The Essential Guide
ISBN 978-1-86144-067-9 £8.99

Dyslexia and Other Learning Difficulties
A Parent's Guide ISBN 978-1-86144-042-6 £8.99

Bullying A Parent's Guide
ISBN 978-1-86144-044-0 £8.99

Epilepsy The Essential Guide
ISBN 978-1-86144-063-1 £8.99

Your First Pregnancy The Essential Guide
ISBN 978-1-86144-066-2 £8.99

Gap Years The Essential Guide
ISBN 978-1-86144-079-2 £8.99

Secondary School A Parent's Guide
ISBN 978-1-86144-093-8 £9.99

Primary School A Parent's Guide
ISBN 978-1-86144-088-4 £9.99

Applying to University The Essential Guide
ISBN 978-1-86144-052-5 £8.99

ADHD The Essential Guide
ISBN 978-1-86144-060-0 £8.99

Student Cookbook – Healthy Eating The Essential Guide
ISBN 978-1-86144-069-3 £8.99

Multiple Sclerosis The Essential Guide
ISBN 978-1-86144-086-0 £8.99

Coeliac Disease The Essential Guide
ISBN 978-1-86144-087-7 £9.99

Special Educational Needs A Parent's Guide
ISBN 978-1-86144-116-4 £9.99

The Pill An Essential Guide
ISBN 978-1-86144-058-7 £8.99

University A Survival Guide
ISBN 978-1-86144-072-3 £8.99

View the full range at **www.need2knowbooks.co.uk**.
To order our titles call **01733 898103**, email **sales@ n2kbooks.com** or visit the website. Selected ebooks available online.

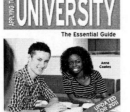

Need - 2 - Know, Remus House, Coltsfoot Drive, Peterborough, PE2 9BF